My Round!

Published in Great Britain by Private Eye Productions Ltd.,
34 Greek Street, London W1.

© 1983 Pressdram Ltd.
Illustrations by George Adamson © 1983.

Designed by Martin Lee.

ISBN 233 97607 8.

Printed by Butler & Tanner Ltd, Frome and London
Typeset by Cold Composition Ltd., Tonbridge.

My Round!

Richard Ingrams & John Wells
Illustrated by George Adamson

PRIVATE EYE

7 MAY 1982

Dear Bill,
I don't know how the Falklands situation looks from your end, but things are certainly pretty hairy here in the Bunker. I think last time I put p. to p. old Haig was still whizzing to and fro on his mission of peace and reconciliation and seemed set to do so for some considerable time to come. Shortly after that however, the old boy rather flaked out, describing the Argies as a bunch of brainless thugs, and was henceforth somewhat persona non grata in the corridors of power. Then little Pym took off in the Concorde to try and sort things out. As far as I could gather he got a pretty good flea in his ear from the Yanks, and was told that Hopalong was far too busy having his wrinkles lifted to bother with his so-called oldest ally.

If this whole episode has demonstrated one thing, Bill, it is that all those years of sucking up to the likes of Hopalong and the chap before whatever his name was who used to walk round holding hands with his wife have been a blind waste of time. I've always held the view that the U.S. were pretty good eighth raters when it came to a scrap, no doubt due to their disgusting drinking habits and having a glass of water put in front of them every time they sit down. As for Hopalong, you know my view: they would think it jolly weird if we had Donald Sinden being Prime Minister instead of the Boss.

However, I digress. M. was pretty livid about Pym getting the bum's rush, and decided to show Hopalong what she was made of. Signal transmitted to this crazy bugger with the scrambled egg all over his hat ic the Fleet, with instructions to get their arse into gear and storm ashore on South Georgia to raise the Jolly Roger. This mission was duly accomplished, whereupon the Boss went ape in front of the TV cameras and the other reptiles, and announced that we had won a famous victory as if it was Trafalgar, exhorting the proles to rejoice.

Personally I couldn't see the point of this. I don't know whether you remember 'Doc' Hoolahan, the Irish medico who used to hang about the Grapes in Burwash, but I met him in the Club the other day, and it transpires that he spent the War in Georgia, having been drummed out of the Merchant Navy.

5

He told me it's a bit of rock a hundred miles long, wind whips through you like a knife, and the only solace to be found is the penguins. As for recapturing it, he said it was about as much use as invading Rockall. I thought of relaying this bit of information to the Supremo, but sensed that in her D-Day mood it might be out of place.

I think the whole grisly business is probably my fault for not speaking out at an earlier stage. I'm naive enough to think that someone in charge must have a glint of intelligence or some idea of what is going on, but they always end up bringing one down to earth with a ghastly bump sooner or later. Eg my mistaken admiration at one stage for Peter Carrington. What Pym and the F.O. Pinkoes repeatedly fail to understand is the nature of Johnny Foreigner. You and I having got our knees brown in the 45 Show, would have spotted a mile off that the Argies weren't going to come to heel just because we waved the big stick. All those mixed races are very excitable, and the moment you start threatening them with GBH they rush out into the streets waving their arms about, setting fire to anything they can lay their hands on, signing on in droves at the recruiting office and giving whatever thug happens to be in power that week-end carte blanche to lead them all to Gory Death.

Add to which the two stupid old sods who work in the propaganda office at the FO have rung up all the reptiles and fed them a lot of tall stories to the effect that Galtieri is a prize piss artist, seldom sober after eleven in the morning—that Costa Bravas is only let out on the end of a flex from the cardiac ward, that all their senior officers dress up as Adolf Hitler in private and torture everything that moves. You could say most of that about our lot.

I'll tell you another funny thing, Bill. You remember when the Polish business blew up I was having a drink with Furniss at the Natwest? Well, I was in there, trying to sort out my possible investment in Maurice's Scandinavian Brick enterprise, and Furniss told me that it's exactly the same all over again. The Argentine is mortgaged up to the hilt, huge loans from the NatWest and most of the others, not the hope of a snowball in hell of getting it back, and if things get any worse it could be Wall Street all over again. I said couldn't they lend their money to sensible people like the Japs who could be relied on to give it back, but he said the Japs had got money coming out of their ears, and at the time it seemed like a

good idea because the Argies were 'buying' a lot of British weaponry, not to mention that aircraft carrier.

To crown it all, we have to put up with a flood of ex-Falklanders coming to the house and telling us to stop sodding about because they're perfectly happy living in Ruislip. I told the Boss that by the time the fighting was over the whole place would be even more uninhabitable than it was before, but she's got her hackles up, and is scanning the popularity polls with a very nasty look in her eye. Saatchis keep telling her that if she sticks at it she's got the next election in the bag, but between you and me, Bill, I think there might be considerable sighs of relief heaved on all sides were we to find ourselves back to square one at Flood Street.

Keep the home fires burning,
Yours aye,

DENIS

Dear Bill,

I do hope you didn't think I was too stand-offish not coming down to Frant for the Sponsor-a-Seawolf Bring and Buy. I'm afraid the Major rather jumped the gun putting my name on the poster. Don't imagine for a moment I'm not sympathetic to your line on biffing the Argie, it's just that when you're at the centre of things matters of this nature do take on rather a different complexion.

I've got rather friendly with old Pym during the last day or two, and I think he's probably quite sound. His point of view is that sooner or later, whatever they say in the talking shop, we've got to hand the sheepshaggers' stomping ground over to the Gauchos, and in the light of that it would seem rather pointless to spend millions of pounds on a full-scale D-Day scenario when it could be quietly earning interest on deposit in the NatWest. I said then why all the fuss in the first place, and he said the Boss had to do something just to show them what for, but as to actually reoccupying the cratered guano depository, it wasn't really on even with the Ghurkas, as they would only get shat on from a considerable height by Galtieri's Flying Circus (and I may say with a good deal more accuracy than by our lot).

Whether the Boss goes along with all this it's hard to say. I told Pym that from my knowledge of the beast she tends to go over the top, often without warning, on the ils ne-passeront-pas routine, e.g. Rhodesia, Mineworkers, etc, however if you sit back having made your point in a reasonable manner, retire behind the lines to the Mess for a quiet pipe and a snort or two, you often find she puts down smoke and sneaks back to a more defensible position when no one's looking.

The danger is, of course, as I outlined to Pym over a large sticky in the dining room while M. was doing one of her Panoramas, is that this Admiral Sandy Whatnot, who is clearly a very jumpy little bugger, may get browned off with steaming round in circles laden down to the gunwales with puking soldiery and decide the best cure for mal de mer is to unload them all into landing crafts and let them take their chance in hand to hand combat with the tin-helmeted gorillas. Pym said there was no chance of that, it was all under very tight control from the hut in Virginia Water, but having seen round said hut and not having been unduly impressed I wouldn't put it past little Sandy to take the law into his own hands.

By the by, have you seen that prize charlie from the MoD who reads out the score on TV? I said to Pym they might get a slightly cheerier cove like for example that friend of the Major's who used to be a Bingo caller. The present incumbent puts me very much in mind of your sky-pilot chum outside Tonbridge during the war who did time following complaints from assorted mothers in the neighbourhood about incidents during lantern slide lectures. Not that I am implying for a moment old Frankenstein is similarly inclined, he just has that same graveyard look and a lack of what Saatchis would call pazam.

I do entirely agree with you about the closet Marxists at the BBC. I've been predicting this for years, but nobody takes a blind bit of notice. There's a very nobby sort of cove in charge now at the Corporation who owns some great pile in Yorkshire which they use for TV commercials. A big fat bloke in striped shirts, he obviously has no idea of the sort of revolutionary reptiles he is harbouring. Anyway he went down to the H of C to argue the toss with some of our rather rougher elements and apparently got his balls chewed off in no uncertain manner. I keep telling the Boss, if ever there was a state owned industry ripe for privatisation, it is that nest of Pinkoes and Traitors at Shepherds Bush. Fifty quid a year they charge now, just so we can watch highlights from the Argentine evening bulletin. And that's an awful lot of snorts in anybody's language. The only thing worth looking at is Wentworth, and I'm sure a private film company could do that just as well.

But I am wandering from the point. At the time of writing, the UN man is banging heads together in New York, and Pym is preparing hearts and minds at this end for a swift twitch of the rug from under the few remaining loyalist sheepshaggers. This is called being flexible. You may have noticed the talk about their wishes being paramount has rather faded on the air and are probably bloody angry about it, but when you see the way these chaps run the show you'd probably be quite grateful to see them climbing down off their warhorses.

9

I hope this doesn't cost us our friendship Bill, but quite honestly I am sick to death of the whole ghastly business. I feel more and more like that very old man who's always on the gogglebox saying he can't wait to turn his toes up. You know the one I mean. Lives near Battle.

Yours in the Lord,

DENIS

10 Downing Street
Whitehall

4 JUNE 1982

Dear Bill,

I'm afraid our Algarve jaunt is going to have to be shelved. As you know, I'd been banking on the war putting paid to Hopalong's State Visit, and I naturally presumed that Old Redsocks would similarly take a hint and stay firmly ensconced in the Vatican. Not but what the Boss isn't giving him a very cold shoulder, especially as he has been trying to stick his oar in on the Falklands. According to Boris this is because all the Argies are RCs and I suppose he feels a duty to stick up for them, dirty little dagoes though you or I might consider them to be. Needless to say Runcie is smarming about the place showing his teeth as per' usual and talking about a merger between the Left Footers and ourselves in the C of E. Not to mention a lot of canoodling and hanky panky for the cameras.

Say what you like about our Polish visitor, he has always struck me as being very sound on buggers and women priests, so how Runcie thinks he can do a deal with him when the Established Church in this country is crawling with both is beyond a man of my limited intellectual powers. I always told M. she made a fundamental error giving Runcie the top job, and Archie Wellbeloved would have filled the bill a darn sight better, even though he doesn't make a lot of sense since his last little skirmish with the Reaper.

Meanwhile the Boss is still in a state of euphoria. Imagine how you or I, Bill, feel after a dozen or so really large ones; the fire in the veins, the light in the eye, the spring in the step, an all-pervading sense of confidence and achievement for no very good reason. She somehow manages to get it all without recourse to the screw cap. Amazing, isn't it? As you know, I've taken rather a back seat on this one, and Pym wasn't any too keen either. However from desultory visits to the Hut where the Brass Hats run the show with their Space Invader machines, I did get the impression that shovelling the boys ashore was by no means a piece of cake and hats off to them. But the question that has been troubling me ever since the kick off, is what happens next? I managed to raise the matter with Brother Nott when he came round to be programmed by the Boss. Nott, en passant, is some kind of tax lawyer, completely out of his depth, and I'm told he was mixed up in the Rossminster business. I am constantly getting him mixed up with Frankenstein who reads out the scores on the TV for the MoD. Anyway, M. being upstairs taking a transfer charge call from her new fancy man, President Mitterand, I took the opportunity of probing our bespectacled friend on the long term scenario. Assuming the Argies run up the White Flag and the sheepshaggers are rehabilitated in their huts, Parish Council re-elected etc, what then? Of course, as usual, it turned out the politicos hadn't given a moment's consideration to such matters. Nott rolled his eyes, shuffled his feet, and burbled away a bit about 'opening the place up'. Biggish garrison, longer airstrip, all the usual guff. He even tried to spin me some yarn about enlisting Jap know-how to harvest the seaweed, which according to the boffins has magical rejuvenating properties. I said where would this leave the sheepshaggers? After all, they'd only gone there for a bit of peace and quiet in the first place, now they'd been bombarded from arsehole to breakfast-table, and here we are talking about erecting seaweed factories.

You know these lawyers, Bill. Nott looked at his watch, burbled away about options and getting round the green baize to thrash it all out, but not a word of sense to be gleaned from his discourse.

You ask what it's all going to cost. According to Boris, who has had a look at Howe's sums, the bill so far is pushing £3,000 million. All of which makes the talk about M3 and the Cuts

look a bit bloody stupid. However, that sort of nonsense has been swept under the rug and Saatchis are talking about a khaki election. If you ask me, they've all got completely carried away and the sooner they sober up and face the music the better it will be for all concerned. Even Pym has taken to wearing red, white and blue underpants and raving on about how we've recovered our national pride. I'm beginning to think Peter Carrington probably got it right in the first place. The FO scheme was to smuggle the whole bang shoot over to the Argies under cover of darkness while everyone was watching Brideshead Revisited on the telly, and if the buffoon Galtieri hadn't jumped the gun with his scrap merchants everything would now be tickety boo. However no one gives a damn what I think so I may as well save my breath to cool my Toddy.

Pax vobiscum,

DENIS

10 Downing Street
Whitehall

Dear Bill,

A lull at long last in the mad rush of distinguished visitors. The Supreme Pontiff has toddled off to try and talk a bit of sense into the Argies, and Old Hopalong has been driven away in his charabanc full of gorillas for his Eight-Capitals of Europe in Four Days Tour. I must say, Bill, I was pretty glad to see the back of him, not to mention his better half. I couldn't make out why they wanted to come here in the first place: I suppose at their age they like to travel a bit and see the sights before they come to hand in the dinner pail, and if so they clearly got their money's worth with a personalised reception by H.M. the Queen and a Disneyland-style ride round the Park with H.R.H. doing his Christmas Card number dressed up as Mr Pickwick. Though I gather the effect was rather spoiled by the heavies following in their armoured car who looked as though they'd got into the wrong film. I sympathised with the Duke afterwards over a stiff one in the gun room, and he said he supposed it was all in a day's work, and they'd had a few good titters backstage at Nancy getting everything arse about face on the etiquette front. I suppose that must be about the only laugh to be had in their line of work.

I was on parade for the big speech scene at Halitosis Hall, fortified I may say by a quart or so of Pimms very kindly laid on by Boris prior to our departure. The heat was stifling, six hundred sweating MPs, old Hailsham sitting there in his horsehair wig scratching himself, all those geriatric Labour peers wheeled out of the Old Folks' Home adjusting their hearing aids. So you can imagine the pong. Then the most amazing thing, Bill. Hopalong finally lopes onto the stage in his corset and full make-up, and blow me, reels off a proper rip-snorter of a tirade lasting the best part of two hours. All very sound, Red Menace to be fought tooth and claw, ancient values, wit and wisdom of old Winston sprinkled in for good measure. Your Rotary at Deal would have lapped it up, and the boss was wriggling about in her seat fair purring with delight. But this is the amazing thing, Bill, the old stager did it all word-perfect without a note in sight. I was absolutely bowled over, and gave a nod of approval to Boris, who had managed to infiltrate the ranks of security men lurking among the floral decorations. He, to my surprise, only tapped his nose in a knowing way and gave me a broad wink. Later when we were shuffling out of the hall, he drew me aside and showed me how it had all been done with mirrors, the speech rolling off a treadle operated by one of Hopalong's handlers, and reflected on a sheet of glass where the old cove could read it with ease, all unbeknownst to his wondering audience, just like they do on the telly. The whole thing's frightfully ingenious and packs up the size of a suitcase. I asked if they could get me one from America for my Rugby dinners, as it would save an awful lot of time and angst if I could get Maurice's smutty jokes off pat rather than having to bugger them up and ask him for the real punch line, thus incurring the bread roll treatment from the Tunbridge Wells brigade.

Meanwhile our lot seem to be getting a good deal of stick behind the scenes over the South Atlantic Farrago. Even Boris is having some difficulty in cracking the telegrams flying to and fro from the Min. of Def. If you ask me M. is anxious to avoid too embarrassingly large a cull of Argies. Hence the dropping of free-offer leaflets, and the midnight phone calls to General Mendoza telling him to come out with his hands up and his trousers round his ankles, all of which as you or I could tell them is an absolute waste of time. The orders from Brer Galtieri are clearly to do or die for the Fatherland, the individual Argie on the spot doesn't know whether he's having a shit or combing his hair, and short of the SAS putting sennapods in their water supply it looks as though a pretty grisly ding dong is on the cards.

I can't see the sense of it myself, and I can't really believe that the sheepshaggers are exactly relishing the prospect of seeing their little wooden homesteads blown to smithereens. Why they wanted to go there in the first place I can't imagine. God knows there are enough uninhabitable islands dotted about our own inshore waters if that's the kind of thing they want. Take for example the Isle of Muck where you may remember I was forced to spend a brief holiday under the roof of the puce-faced old miser, Lord Margolis or whatever he was called, while Margaret bagged the grouse.

Meanwhile, taking advantage of the diversion, friend Begin has decided to go on one of his wogbashing sprees. He never learns his lesson. It's just like Space Invaders, the harder you hit them the more the little buggers come buzzing in. I was having a bit of a jaw about it all with Furniss down at the NatWest. I put it to him, over a second bottle of Amontillado, that it struck me as odd we should get our knickers in a knot about single figure inflation when the Israelites are into telephone numbers: yet here they are mounting an MGM spectacular with no thought to the cost. Could it be, as with Poland and Argentina, that I was indirectly subsidising this with no hope of any return through the good offices of the National Westminster Bank? Furniss had another swig of his filing cabinet lubricant, gave a rueful chuckle, and said not guilty on this occasion, the whole show is kept on the road by Marks and Sparks and other well-wishers about the globe who pass the hat round come Jewish Christmas or whatever they call it.

Talking of which, Parkinson tells me that our own Party Funds have taken a very nice little upswing since the scrap merchants raised the flag. The only cloud, it seems to me, on M's horizon, is that Worzel might decide after all to jack it in and go back to the second hand bookshops. However I'm sure his wife will keep his nose to the grindstone. I'm told she wears the trousers.

Hasta la Vista, amigo mio,

DENIS

15

10 Downing Street
Whitehall
2 JULY 1982

Dear Bill,

It seems as though I misjudged the temper of the Argies on the question of Menendez' Last Stand. As you probably saw on the gogglebox they ran up the white flag pretty smartish following the usual negotiations from a callbox, since when the Boss has been on Cloud Nine and shows no signs of coming down to earth, despite the fact that Brother Weighell and all the other Union Jackasses are playing sillybuggers again and the country has virtually ground to a halt.

Nonetheless the Old Girl's confidence seems well based. Having popped over for a brief champagne celebration with old Hopalong, she is now back and planning a Victory Parade not to mention her own visit to the newly reconquered territories to receive the homage of the grateful sheepshaggers, all fifty-nine of them. I should say that I am being pressed to pose for a photocall at the Bar of the Upland Goose, but quite frankly going that distance for a drink when there's not even so much as a clock golf course and they're all half cuckoo and cross-eyed is not my idea of a lark. Argentina I am told is quite a different kettle of fish. Batty Dugdale's uncle had quite a decent handicap and he spoke very highly of the courses there, no shortage of caddies and some very sound buffers in the Clubhouse.

Worzel misjudged the public mood yet again by trying to make mischief with the help of some Conservative activist woman from Gerrard's Cross. The reptiles dredged up a letter this old bag had addressed to Margaret on the eve of the Argie Invasion, to which M. had replied that as far as we were concerned fifteen marines armed with catapults and one Alsatian dog were quite sufficient to keep the gauchos off the guano, everything tickety boo etc. Of course at the time this was perfectly true, and anyway like all these letters it wasn't actually written by Margaret in the first place, but cobbled up by one of Carrington's minor weirdoes at the FO. This didn't stop the smelly socks side, including the old salt Jim Callaghan, from trying to make capital out of it. Needless to say the moment things started to look ugly the Boss fired off

one of her Exocet ripostes, pointing out that Worzel, if he'd been in charge would have done bugger all and left the sheepshaggers to their fate. No bad thing Bill, entre nous, but one can't really say that in public—and the Opposition front bench blew up as per usual and was sunk without trace in a matter of seconds.

The real, juggling act, as you will appreciate, is how to keep the Falklands spirit fresh when Sid Weighell and co are doing their damnedest to introduce a note of reality. Luckily the Palace have come to M's assistance by delivering the bouncing baby boy bang on cue, thus giving rise to further flag-waving and patriotic outbursts.

The Dartmouth woman I gather was told to keep her head down, though old Spencer bumbled about doing his dotty earl bit for the TV cameras which always goes down very well with the lower orders. Margaret, inevitably, wanted to be in on it, and I think Saatchis were angling for a shot of her on the balcony holding the baby, but HM put her foot down. Personally I couldn't get too excited about it all: if you've seen one baby you've seen them all, but far be it from me to sneer at any excuse to bring out the bubbly, and I toddled round to Buck House with M. on the happy day to sample the Moet and have a bit of a jaw with the D of E. He agreed with me a hundred per cent about the sheepshaggers, said it was a Godforsaken spot and now they'd got three thousand randy marines roaming about down there for good he didn't give the breed much chance of survival in any recognisable form.

I am sorry to hear about Maurice's troubles. The SDP was always a pretty dodgy line in my view, not that that is any reason for turning the gas on. Did he realise this North Sea stuff wasn't toxic? However the explosion can have done him no good and I'll do my best to go and see him at the Bin as soon as the weather gets better. I hope he's in a fit state to mark his card for the Men's Singles between Fatso and Dr. Kildare. What a prize pair of twats! Apparently old Fatso's stock has gone straight through the floor. He seems really out of his element at Halitosis Hall and sat out the hostilities on the back benches arms crossed without a word escaping his lips, whereas the keen young Doctor was constantly on his feet, having learned off yards of the UN Charter by heart, precious little use though that was, so he could pip the old gastronome at the post. Not but what Owen isn't quite clearly a vicious greaser, the kind of interfering little houseman you often find in clinics who tells you to take a grip of yourself, cut out the booze and fags and live as miserable an existence as he quite obviously does. The only time he ever showed any signs of humanity was when he tried to strangle that Trot student who was throwing rotten tomatoes at him.

See you at Gatwick,
Yours in anticipation,

DENIS

10 Downing Street
Whitehall
30 JULY 1982

Dear Bill,
I presume you are now back in the country. I do apologise for my no show at Gatwick, but I was creeping out at the crack of dawn with the clubs and tropical kit when the Boss flung open the door of her operations room where she had been at work since half past four, confiscated my travellers' cheques and British Caledonian documents, and said there was no question of my going away while our gallant lads were still trickling back from the South Atlantic. Presence was required in the quayside with Union Jack bowler, 'Welcome' balloons, poised to join in the Chorus of Land of Hope and Glory. I hope nonetheless that Florida was a success and that you managed to find someone to go round with.

As you may gather from the above, every effort is still being made by Saatchis to wring the last possible drop out of the Falklands. It is already being repeated as a major drama series by the BBC, Runcie has been roped in to give thanks in St. Paul's, and various showbiz johnnies have been persuaded to appear in gala performances of the Royal Tournament. As if this were not enough in the way of Good Cheer, Murray's Smelly Socks came to heel and clobbered little Buckton without Margaret so much as raising a finger, the first time

I've seen any sense out of that lot since the General Strike. You can imagine that even I was less depressed than usual at the way things were looking. To crown it all, no invitation from the Isle of Muck, so prospects seemed bright for two weeks of relative p and q at the country flat down at Lamberhurst. However, in the words of Shakespeare, the best laid plans often run amuck.

As I may have said before Whitelaw is a perfectly decent old bean who likes the sauce as much as any of us, but he is totally out of his depth in the modern world. You've probably seen all the sniggering in the gutter press about this mad navvy who climbed into bed with the Queen. They'd scarcely got over that one when the top royal minder, one Commander Trestletable, was caught out by the reptiles with his pants down carrying on with some bumboy in his leisure hours. Crikey, Bill, all hell was let loose. Uproar at Halitosis Hall. Heads must roll. Poor old Oystereyes put in to bat by the Boss goes down under a hail of body-liners, and with a cry of 'Leggo, you rotters', retires to drown his grief in Members' Bar where he is seen sitting head in hands, his huge frame shaking with uncontrollable sobs. I must say if I were him, Bill, I'd have thrown in the sponge long ago and sodded off pdq to the little shooting lodge in the Lake District.

Personally I couldn't understand why on earth our chaps were getting their knickers in such a twist. Anybody who's ever put foot in Buck House has seen the kind of thing that goes on. You probably remember the time the Major was taken short at that Garden Party and stumbled across a couple of guardsmen in the shrubbery. When I was last in the Superintendent's office looking for a little more soda the smell of cheap perfume was quite overpowering, and there were a couple of sailors being royally entertained who as far as I could see had come straight in off the street. I have indeed frequently raised the topic with the D of E, who lines up with you and me on the Gay Question having seen a thing or two in the Navy, but he says that even in George the Sixth's time the place was crawling with wooftahs of every size and shape, number one culprit being the old Queen Mother who makes a point of employing nothing but bumbandits and brownhatters in every possible post. Blunt, as the Duke says, was only the icing on the cake.

All in all the reptiles are suddenly having a field day: corruption in the Met, as if we hadn't all known about that; secrets leaking out of Cheltenham, as if there were any left; even muttering about similarities with the last days of old whisker-chops Macmillan, who also had some duffer at the Home Office who didn't know his arse from his elbow. If you ask me there's a lot of spite involved. Margaret herself says, and I must say I agree with her, they can't bear the sheer brilliance of the Falklands Show, and are just trying to throw mud in the hope that something will stick. There are even some real swine suggesting that the whole exercise needn't have happened in the first place. Fortunately Joe Public is not so easily duped, and Saatchi's Market Research suggests that we are streets ahead of poor old Worzel, who now scores minus four, the lowest since Hitler.

On a more serious topic, I see that Lillywhite's have got a summer sale on. Do you want me to get you one of those electric barbeque trolleys that Daphne hankered after when we stayed with your friends near Lisbon? (hadn't they come unstuck on intensive pig rearing?) I think there's something like £99.99 off, which in these days of hardship and recession is not be sniffed at. I managed to drop in on Maurice last week, by the way, and he was sitting up in bed, though not making much sense. Apparently they've given him those happy pills, and he is trying to join BUPA retrospectively.

Hasta la vista, as the Argie said when he saw Johnny Gurkha coming for him with his cutlass.

Yours aye,

DENIS

10 Downing Street
Whitehall

13 AUGUST 1982

Dear Bill,

I can't remember whether I missed the post last time over the St. Paul's Thanksgiving affair. Saatchis had planned the whole thing as a major boost for the Boss, full coverage on the telly, Royal Family filling the front pews, herald trumpeters, fanfares, Old Contemptibles wheeled out, Worzel in his donkey jacket shifting about uneasily in row Z. Somewhere along the way, however, the whole thing came unstuck. As I may have said before one of the Boss's biggest-ever mistakes was appointing that silly bugger Runcie to the C of E hot seat. Over and over again at the time I stressed the merits of old Archie Wellbeloved, and over and over again I was told not to talk nonsense. Even in the state he is at present, plugged into all kinds of wires and apparatus, Archie would have laid on a better show than the grinning chimpanzee from Canterbury.

I had taken the precaution of ingesting a few pretty stiff ones across the road in the Barbican Arms, and my recollection of the opening moments is not all that clear, but I realised as soon as the Proprietor made her entrance, in total silence without so much as a breath of applause, let alone the massed trumpeters or Cup Final cheering we had expected, that someone had blundered. When Runcie finally minced up into the pulpit and adjusted his frock, instead of rendering thanks to the great Bartender in the Sky for the sinking of the Belgrano and all his other mercies viz unexploded bombs, crass bungling by Argies, massacre at Goose Green etc, we got a lecture, would you believe, on the evils of war with the strong suggestion the whole episode need not have happened (Of course he may well be right, but that was not the time or the place to say so.) M. inevitably was fit to be tied, shredded her programme, looked at her watch several times during the homily, and when it came to shaking hands with the Primate at the West Door, gave him a radioactive look that left him smouldering.

If you ask me, Bill, the C of E is entirely up the spout. The latest news, as you may have seen in the Telegraph, is that they've re-written the National Anthem so as not to offend the Argies, another of friend Runcie's little wheezes. The next thing you know it'll be women priests. Didn't Daphne put herself down on the waiting list at one stage, or am I mixing her up with Maurice's old flame from AA? I know the Major got mixed up with some frightful harpy who went in for speaking with tongues after she'd had a few.

Bad news about interest rates. As usual the Boss and Howe are over the moon about it, light at the end of the tunnel etc., but as I said to little Furniss at the NatWest when I went down to assess the damage, it's one in the eye for decent hardworking chaps like you and me and Maurice who have put something away for a rainy day. To cap it all, having proffered what he terms a schooner of Amontillado, i.e. a thimbleful of vile-smelling expectorant, Furniss breaks the further glad tidings that the NatWest in its infinite wisdom, having sunk most of our deposit accounts in Poland and Argentina, has now advanced a massive loan to some little mafia chap, sometime banker to the Vatican, recently found dangling under Blackfriars Bridge with a heavy brick in his Y fronts.

I am very glad to hear that Maurice is out and about. I passed on to little Geoffrey Howe the cri de coeur of a small businessman with a lifetime of experience in double glazing

and export contacts in the Middle East, and the message of cheer from the Treasury is that HP restrictions are being lifted; the logic behind this being that as people haven't got any money, they should be encouraged to get themselves as deeply into debt as possible by lashing out on three piece suites, a second refrigerator, and microwave ovens. Double-glazing is therefore due for a boom, ditto Maurice's brick contraption, though the last I heard of that, when he was coming to in the Home, writs were being issued for infringing the Swedish patent.

The latest for the Buckton treatment are the floorswabbers at the NHS. According to the Boss and that little creep Fowler they've been offered a very decent three per cent, which may not be a great deal on the amount they're earning at present, but you can't have everything in this life, at least they can't, and Margaret has obviously spotted another soft target for her salami treatment on the Unions. Personally I can't help feeling a twinge of sympathy for them. Maurice had two very nice little male nurses holding him down when I went to visit him in the Bin and knowing the old boy I doubt very much whether he left them any kind of gratuity when he finally discharged himself through the window.

We are now off to Switzerland, to stay with one of Margaret's old chums in a moated grange. It is slightly preferable to the Isle of Muck, but only just. The widow Glover is not one of life's merrier souls, and I have asked Boris to load one false bottom in my suitcase with the necessary emergency supplies. In my experience all you ever get in the Alps is some ghastly sticky made out of rotting Edelweiss.

Ski heil, alte Freund, and yodel-ho he ho.

DENIS

27 AUGUST 1982

c/o Frau Glover
Schloss Bangelstein
Birchermuesli
Switzerland

Dear Bill,
I wonder whether you got my PC from the airport. Not much time to scribble more than a line as I was rather under the eagle eye and thought the joke about the mountain goat might be deemed in poorish taste.

As I foresaw, high life at the Schloss is uneventful, to say the very least. The whole idea was for the Boss to put her feet up and get the Falklands out of her system once and for all, but as usual it hasn't quite worked out like that on the ground. She gets up every morning well before dawn, buggering people in England about and running up an immense phone bill for the Widow, Boris the while being dispatched to the local W.H. Schmidt to bring back all the English papers, these being an average of two days late, though you couldn't tell that from looking at them, and costing £1.50 a go. Then more ringing up, endless heaps of official letters, autographed pictures and the like to be carried down to the Postamt by Boris.

There follows a frugal repast — apple juice, black bread and ten varieties of cheese, and if I'm lucky a thimbleful of some Alpine sticky out of a cut glass horror in a wicker basket that plays The Sound of Music at a deafening level of decibels if one so much as brushes one's hand against it, thus putting an effective stop to any nocturnal forays.

The afternoon is given over to motor excursions, when M. and I are allowed out sandwiched-between several burly Swiss detectives in the back seat of the Glover Rolls, the Widow comfortably ensconced in front beside her very elderly chauffeur Hanfstaengel, drawing our attention to the various peaks on the horizon. Matterhorn, Schmatterhorn, when you've seen one you've seen them all.

On one occasion I made the mistake of suggesting we stop at a roadside hostelry of fretted wood with waitresses in embroidered pinafores. It took a bit of time to find seats for all the detectives, but when things settled down and the Boss was busy with her giant aerosol "taking out" the wasps I managed to obtain the drinks list, four foot square and all in Bosche, from one of the frauleins. Inevitably I ended up with a glass filled a good six inches over the top with vivid green chunks of pineapple, chocolate, nuts and a paper parasol on top. Alcoholic content nil per cent. Hanfstaengel and the Heavies in the meantime lowering their bulbous noses into bottomless stone mugs with little metal lids.

As dusk falls, Herr Zwingli, the gloomier half of the Widow's live-in couple, appears with further trays laden with apple juice and dried fruit to draw the curtains and switch on a forty-eight inch colour TV, given over to the preliminary heats of the Eurovision Yodelling Knock-Out, interviews with incomprehensible goatherds and lengthy reports — keenly studied by the Widow G. — from the Zurich Stock Market on the movement of the Swiss Franc against the Yen. After this, an early bed in my carved cot under the low rafters, where I toss miserably to and fro wrestling with one of those ghastly giant eiderdowns filled with duck feathers, comes as a positive relief.

In contrast to my own somewhat disconsolate condition, the Boss remains on a level of intolerable euphoria, particularly at the recent polls showing Worzel and Fatso in the doghouse. She drones on to the Widow about her plans for the next fifteen years, how she's got the Health Workers in a

hammerlock, interest rates tumbling, inflation bottoming out, everything in the garden lovely. She was particularly tickled, as I may say I was too, about the news from Dublin. As you probably observed from your seat in the back stalls, we had been having quite a bit of stick of late from the slippery little bugger called the Teasock, Charlie Haughey. Quite apart from his refusal to smoke out the Mad Bombers holed up in Dublin, he then went and stabbed us in the back over the Falklands, declining to support the boycott and demanding the Boss be arraigned at the Hague for violation of human rights, or something along those lines. Well, God is not mocked, I always say, and now it turns out that one of his chief advisors, the Attorney General, has been offering bed and board to some kind of mad axeman. Not having been born yesterday, you and I obviously have a pretty shrewd idea of what was up. You remember the retired bank manager in Folkestone — Macintosh? Radmore? — anyway, no matter — who was always trying to put Borstal Boys on the straight and narrow and getting his hi-fi equipment stolen for his pains. Thank goodness Sir M. Havers is a bird of another feather.

I took the liberty of suggesting to Margaret that she might take the opportunity, while little Haughey is off his guard, of launching a surprise attack on Dublin in emulation of Brother Begin, but the idea was not well received.

You notice that Pinko Prior waited until the cat was away before putting the boot in on unemployment. I used rather to admire his pluck in standing up to the Boss, but I imagine a year in exile among the mad Orangemen has taken its toll. If you ask me, poor old Whitelaw was never the same after his spell on the Bogside.

If you see Maurice, tell him I spent four hours in some dreadful Bierstube near Geneva Station, listening to relays of grinning zither players, waiting for his double-glazing contact Kornfield to turn up. A very elderly barmaid who had a smattering of English told me that someone of that name had been arrested the afternoon before and taken off in handcuffs, but it may not have been the same person.

Next stop Balmoral. Another milestone on the dreadful road.

Yours aye

DENIS

BALMORAL CASTLE
ABERDEENSHIRE   **TEL.BALLATER 3**
SCOTLAND   **STATION: BALLATER**

Dear Bill,

So here we are, doing our annual penance in the great gothic pile. Usual crowd, various Royal throwbacks, chinless sprigs of the aristocracy, and the stray coon basking in the conservatory. Good deal of gossip behind the green baize door to the effect that the Phillipses aren't getting on too well. I asked old Mrs. Donaldson who very kindly came in to run a flat iron over my plus fours after we'd been rained out on the links if there was any truth in it, and she muttered somewhat cryptically in her thick highland brogue that folks like me 'didna ken the half of it' and that 'puir Captain Phillips couldna have been all there in the first place'.

You ask how the Boss is recovering from her little op. The medics were absolutely bowled over by the speed with which she leapt up from the table, the anaesthetic scarcely worn off before she'd asked for the phone on a trolley and was ringing up Howe to blast him out of his holiday flatlet. I had a word afterwards with one of the sawbones, who I think you may once have seen being carried out of the bar at the Major's club. Name of Montague-Brown, or it may be Ribling, lives near Basingstoke and breeds whippets in his spare time, of which he seems to have a good deal, drives a very nice red Roller complete with TV set, cocktail cabinet etc and is very sound on the COHSE layabouts. He feels they should all be gassed and I must say I agree with him. A propos the Boss's miracle recovery, he said he'd never come across a case like it, is thinking of writing to the Lancet and reassures me that it could all be dealt with out of Margaret's BUPA.

You see poor old Nott has finally cracked and decided to quit. Personal reasons was what they said on the wireless, but if you ask me after the Falklands blew up and it transpired that if it had happened a few months later all we'd have had to send was a couple of vomit-stained Sealink ferries and the wreck of the Mary Rose, the Boss had made it pretty clear to him that he'd better hang on, as there had to be someone to carry the can if it all got cocked up but after that he was free to bugger off back to his daffodil farm. Apparently the little fellow had been hankering after Howe's job, though why anyone in their right mind should want that bed of nails being bounced up and down on by the Boss night and day beats me.

Personally, I never had much time for Brother Nott. He's some kind of city lawyer who I am told was mixed up in the Rossminster business. Anyway he always looked pretty out of place shinning down a rope onto the heaving deck to welcome back the Boys in Blue. Altogether a very gloomy streak of piss and I shall not be sorry to see the back of him. I don't know who the hell they'll find to preside over our dwindling divisions, but I imagine Margaret has got some little creep up her sleeve.

Hopalong's been on the blower a lot during the last day or two and getting his ear well and truly chewed off by M. The Russkies are building some big sewage works to dump all their effluent into Lake somewhere or other. Hopalong has got into one of his Shoot out at OK Corral moods and wants us to cut off their spare parts. Normally the Boss can't resist any chance of persecuting the Russian Bear, but on this occasion with 98% unemployment in the West of Scotland and the septic tank manufacturers J. Brown & Co being very loyal subscribers to the Tory kitty, the line has somewhat changed. Our word is our bond. Hopalong's demand for a boycott deeply offensive. Brezhnev a decent old cove when you get to know him etc. Boris, who at the time of writing has the job of exercising the Royal dogs is very cock a hoop about the whole shebang.

What else is new? As I foresaw the latest poll suggests that the Falklands Factor is on the wane, so Saatchis are doing their damnedest to kick a bit of life back into it. The latest wheeze is for some kind of Victory Parade with captured Argies led in chains around the Barbican, contingents of grateful sheepshaggers, Johnny Gurkha riding on a special Daily Telegraph float, hooded SAS veterans parachuting out of the sky trailing smoke and a simulated Exocet attack on the GLC. The latter was my own suggestion, unfortunately vetoed by Nott on the grounds of expense. Another good reason for him to get the boot.

As usual, wetting one's whistle in this miserable mausoleum is proving an uphill task to say the very least. Fortunately the Queen Mother has a secret supply, and during the Charades last night she led me away to an old gun room where we quaffed some very acceptable Highland Fling Malt Whisky she

keeps in an old croquet box. She told me a priceless story about Noel Coward and Lord Mountbatten on holiday in Tangiers which involved a visit to a Turkish Bath and the British Ambassador losing his trousers, but it was rather late and neither of us was too clear in our grasp of detail.

On re-reading the above, it all seems a bit pointless but it may serve to give you some insight into how we pass the time as the rain buckets down and the stags peer in at the windows.

Here's looking at ye.

DENIS

Dear Bill,

Forgive the fragrant rice paper, but it's all they provide you with.

I can't remember whether you've ever been to the Land of the Rising Sun, but it takes a bit of getting used to after Tunbridge Wells. To begin with there aren't any numbers on the houses, and even with a phrase book it's very hard to make oneself understood. As you may have gathered from the Telegraph, the name of the game on this trip is to try and persuade Mr Yamaha, the Head Nip, to stem the flood of Hondas, Datsuns and other miracles of modern technology into the British Isles, and in exchange to spend several billion yen on importing the Michael Edwards Junk Collection. Another wheeze is for one of their big Video operations to set up shop in Toxteth or somewhere like that, thus solving unemployent at a stroke. As usual the Foreign Office has come up with an absolute stumblebum non-starter. The only things we make that the Japs want to import are various pansy products like Fairisle liberty bodices and Fortnum and Mason jam cosies, and can you imagine the workshy yobboes in the outer darkness responding to Changi-style discipline and the crack of the stock-whip? The Boss and I having just returned from a Space Invader factory on the outskirts, I can tell you Len Murray would have a fit. 05.45 clock in, 05.46 ritual obeisance to image of the Chairman, Mr Y.K. Bonzai, singing of National Anthem, five hundred press-ups, and off they waddle for a fourteen hour shift on a handful of dried seaweed and a tin mug of herbal tea, under the watchful eye of the TV cameras, and woe betide any slacker who fails to achieve his regulation output of 25 Space Invaders by the end of it.

The Boss was absolutely bowled over by the whole thing but I think even she realises that John Bull might be wriggling under the wire if they tried it at British Leyland. And who can blame him, say I.

I managed to miss the banquet at the Mitsubishi Bank last night, pleading hypertension and sore feet, and made contact with your old chum 'Harpic' Connolly, who I gather was already fairly far gone when he came out here. He's now a rep for some American Whisky firm, and certainly looks the part. He turned up in the hotel lobby wearing a suit and sandals with a presentation pack of samples for me to savour before we hit the town. He then conducted me to his gas guzzler and we drove out into the neon-lit nightmare. Our first port of call was one of these twenty-four hour fully automatic golf courses, all blazing with floodlights, clusters of nips padding to and fro in shiny boots on the astroturf, barely room to swing a club, all with many an "Ah-so" and an oriental oath, balls whizzing hither and yon like bullets. Give me Huntercombe on a wet afternoon any day. I drew the line at nine holes, especially as Harpic was seeing double by that stage and slicing the ball very badly meanwhile shouting abuse at the injured Nips and throwing their tartan hats into the air-conditioning.

We took refuge in the nineteenth, which was decorated roughly in the style of a Munich beercellar, and who should we run into but poor old Ginger Watkins? Leg in plaster after an accident in the revolving door of an umbrella factory in Kyoto, but glass eye agleam and raring to go to one of these Massage Parlours he'd read about on the plane. Harpic said he knew just the place, and after a few little cups of Japanese tea, a pretty lethal brew apparently made out of fermented bamboo shoots, we climbed into Harpic's convertible and traced an erratic course through the speeding traffic to the Forbidden City, though it all looked much the same to me, especially by night. Harpic assured us that he knew the way, but it became pretty obvious after a while that he hadn't the remotest clue and was badly lost.

By no means discouraged, he drew up outside a luridly lit establishment called the Golden Cock Geisha Palace and we all piled in, Harpic tossing the keys to an impassive attendant who drove off into the night. Smiling ladies plastered in make-up and wearing Madame Butterfly outfits then ushered us into a dimly-lit saloon where we were expected to squat on the floor and cram our legs under a sawn off table while the giggling ladies shuffled away carrying our jackets, spectacles and shoes, returning after about half and hour with three face flannels soaked in boiling hot water and two roses floating in a shaving bowl.

The words snort and snifter, it eventually dawned on us,

meant little to these Oriental handmaidens, whose grasp of English only ran to telling us the show would be beginning in a few minutes. A good while later the lights went out altogether, and two women in pink kimonos came on with fans, swaying to the rhythm of a few old gongs and the usual chopstick music. By this time both Ginger and Harpic were beginning to get a bit restless, shouting a lot about Knocky Knocky, and throwing their flannels at the ladies. This did not turn out to be a good idea as we were immediately given the bum's rush by ten plain clothes Samurai warriors and unable to find the way in again.

Two more days of this insanity and we are off to rub shoulders with Hu Flung Dung who is proposing to do a Galtieri on us over Hong Kong. I'll keep you informed.

Sayonara Blitish Pig.

DENIS

PS I looked round the supermarket for one of those electric backscratchers for Daphne but they said they were out of them.

METROPOLE HOTEL
BRIGHTON

Dear Bill,
So the nightmare begins all over again. I can never make out which is worse, Blackpool or Brighton. In Blackpool the proles predominate, but nowadays Brighton isn't a great deal better: very seedy and run down, a high percentage of wooftahs, crooked antique dealers and superannuated hippies mooching about leaving a wake of hypodermics littering the promenade behind them. Nothing to send home to mother except eighth rate dirty postcards and false teeth made out of icing sugar.

Even so I'd rather be here than the Crown Colony. The pong out there has to be smelt to be believed, Bill. Of course there are about five hundred million of them crammed onto this tiny little island all guzzling their beanshoots and playing mah-jong round the clock, and it is very humid. Also a lot of fat cats being pulled round in gold plated rickshaws, making a pretty penny out of the malodorous hordes, all hoping that the status quo ante will be preserved when the lease runs out and everything reverts to Comrade Dung.

I could tell at a glance when we touched down at the Airport of a Thousand Blossoms in Peking, despite the million dancing children waving their Stars and Stripes and the beaming geriatrics gathered on the red carpet, that friend Dung had no intention of foregoing his rights to the Kowloon Goldmine. What really got Margaret's goat was this little monkey called Sir K P Nuts or some such who smuggled himself aboard the aeroplane and gatecrashed all the summit conferences, grinning and rubbing his hands, revealing half a million quids' worth of gold teeth, and making out he'd been invited by both sides. It emerged that Sir K P along with all the other sleeker Chinks from the Island were banking on M. giving Dung the Falklands treatment, with themselves in the role of the gallant sheepshaggers. However I think even the Boss realised that it was a bit pointless asking Sir Sandy Whatsisname to take on several billion signed up members of the Yellow Peril swarming over the hill in wave after wave with bloodcurdling screams and all able to exist on a grain of rice a week.

As usual the Foreign Office cocked up the whole thing. We left Peking garlanded with opium poppies, plastered out of our minds after five hundred toasts in some sort of pretty lethal Chinese rice sticky, wall to wall grins and bonhomie, only to find a telegram from Dung when we got back to Honkers saying Go Home Capitalist Pigs All This Is Ours By Right We Will Roll You Flat. So if I were you I'd get out of the Hong Kong Shanghai Bank PDQ and put it on the gee-gees. Don't whatever you do invest it with the Natwest because they'll only give it to the Argies and other assorted South American bankrupts.

On the Home Front M. is hoping for an easyish ride this week in the Floral Hall. Saatchis have told everyone to mention the Falklands and Wedgwood Benn as often as possible: new spirit abroad, inflation well under control, wage settlements within three per cent, general cheer about the way the Smelly Socks brigade have espoused permanent revolution and mayhem at Blackpool, no move to oust Worzel so Question Time still a doddle for the forseeable future, all the Trots alive and kicking whatever they now call themselves.

I'm just off via the laundry lift and the underground car park for a toddle round the greens at Pyecombe with poor old Podmore, who has been let out on parole to give the male nurses a bit of a break. I know I said I'd do anything for the cause but stuck up on that platform under the hot lights for two hours with that awful slob Lawson unfolding his thoughts on gas prices seems to me beyond the call of duty. I slipped a tenner to one of the desk clerks here to wear a spare pair of my specs and occupy my seat on the platform.

See you at the Twickers Reunion on the fifteenth.

TTFN

DENIS

10 Downing Street
Whitehall

Dear Bill,

Grim tidings about the interest rates coming down. Furniss broke the news to me when I dropped in to get a new cheque book on my way to the Club. Very apologetic, sherry to hand, and as usual no explanation of the wide gap between the ten percent to the borrowers and the six percent to the wise virgins i.e. you and me. I don't mind admitting I tore into him on the topic of Mexico, Poland and the Argies Dictatorship, but he laid his arm round my shoulders, gave me that shifty smile of his and began to talk about his chrysanthemums which apparently won some of sort of prize at the Datchet Show. Howe keeps urging me to go into National Savings, but I'm buggered if I'm going to give him my money to squander on new by-passes for juggernauts just to boost the standing of that grizzly little streak of piss David Howell.

Did you see we had all the Top Brass round for a hot meal? The idea, according to Saatchis, was to keep the Falklands uppermost in the public mind pending the next election. As far as I could gather, most of them spent the whole show yomping to and fro from the bar at Virginia Water. I didn't know who half of them were, although I did recognise old Dracula face from the Min of Def who used to read out the scores on the box. He seemed to have smartened himself up for the occasion, and was obviously a bit miffed about not getting a gong. Apparently some people were also exercised about poor old Sam Salt not getting anything, but as I said to little Nott, if you start dishing out decorations to everybody whose ship sinks where would it end?

By the way, did you happen to see Nott's fracas with Sir Robin Day on the telly? I missed it, following a rather heavy evening's imbibing with Podmore and his friends from the Home at a little club in Hove, but apparently he got very shirty when Day called him a here today and gone tomorrow sort of chap, unplugged the mike and minced out in a huff. I've never had much time for Day myself, far too pleased with himself if you ask me, very self opinionated, loud voice, wears those common-looking bow ties from Burtons, but I thought on this occasion it was perfectly fair comment and revealed what an unbalanced little pratt Nott really is. According to that rather daft baronet friend of Sticky's who's in merchant banking, Nott has decided to hop it before the Rossminster solids hit the air conditioning. I just pass it on for what it's worth — probably about a hundred grand in the High Court the way things are going these days, so don't put it about.

A propos the Falklands gongs, the Boss was spitting tintacks as you probably saw because the reptiles jumped the gun and broke the embargo. According to the scenario worked out by Saatchis, the idea was to get maximum coverage of the Party Conference, final wind-up speech by the Boss followed by general last night of the Proms jubilation, Union Jack bog rolls being thrown about etc., monopolising the prints, and then as a 'grand climax' let loose the gongs on the Monday morning, flattening the SDP. As it turned out M. had a pretty grisly night with that gag-writer johnny with the long cigarette holder and padded dressing gown, dishing up one bum one-liner after another, then Hopalong's magic mirror prompting device started working sideways half way through and put up the racing results. So when to cap it all the VC's started dribbling onto the front pages the following day, no wonder she hit the ceiling.

Anyway morale was restored by the big march past in the City a few days later. This had all been laid on to make up for Runcie's flopperoo at St Paul's which sounded entirely the wrong note and was dreamed up by a lot of conchie skypilots of the type you always find lurking about having a cigarette in the vestry. The Boss was very carried away, burst into tears, VE Day all over again. Personally I thought it was all a bit pointless, but I suppose if Brother Scargill gets up to his pranks it's nice to know the Army can now be counted on to restore order. The only good laugh of the day was old Worzel on the saluting base in a suit. Shades of the Cenotaph, what?

By the way, I couldn't help feeling a surge of sympathy for poor old H.M on the Prince Andrew front. Having had enough trouble with my own gangling great yob of a son and heir gallivanting around with various unspeakable bits of fluff, pursued by a horde of reptiles and bringing the family name into disrepute, I did think of giving her a bell when it came out that Randy Andy was shacked up in his aunt's tropical love nest with this ghastly stripper called Koo. Boris however

advised against it on the grounds that relations with Bu
House are strained as of late. Apparently H.M. doesn't like
another woman getting in on the act and keeps the Boss
standing to attention throughout their weekly pow-pows,
never even offering her as much as a large Scotch.

Maurice is very euphoric about the Stock Market and is
thinking of going public with Picbrick. I don't know whether
you heard he set the chimney on fire at the Walmsleys'
housewarming, so I wouldn't have thought it was the soundest
of moves, but when he's on a high there's not much you can do
to stop him. Did you see him at the SDP Conference not
making very much sense about the Unions and getting the red
light treatment from the woman with the messy hair? I thought
it was a mistake to call him so soon after the lunch break, but I
don't expect they've got the measure of him yet.

Tootleoo

DENIS

5 NOVEMBER 1982

Dear Bill,

Thank you for your congratulatory suspendergram on the occasion of King Arthur's defeat in the Miners' ballot. The lady who was meant to sing the message of goodwill had rather a nasty cold, so they sent a little old man instead, who didn't have quite the same impact, but at least I was spared his embrace.

As you say it couldn't have happened to a nastier man. Scargill had been whizzing up and down the country waving the red flag at mass rallies, throwing his arms about like an overweight pop singer, telling the workers to rise and throw off their chains, seeing himself I think as a cross between Joan of Arc and Lenin, instead of which they've very sensibly concentrated their minds on keeping up the payments on their videos and deep freezes etc and told him to vanish up his own black hole.

This has obviously given Margaret a tremendous fillip, not to mention the bye-election results this week. I wish I could be more encouraging to Maurice about his own prospects with the SDP, but I fear he's going to come a terrible cropper at Sevenoaks on the big day. I told him they made a big mistake in electing Fatso Jenkins as their commander in chief. I used to see him round the place a bit when he was our man in Brussels, and I must say I found him a tremendous pain. I remember running into him late one night when he was hanging around outside the Study at Number Ten waiting for the green light to come on, and thought the least thing I could do was offer him a snifter. Expressed polite interest in the contents of the drinks cabinet, stocked as always with every conceivable type of snort and sticky, including Boris's mother's plum vodka, and said all he really wanted was a glass of red wine. Net result, little Cosgrove who was on duty that night in the pantry had to pound down to the Pakistani cash and carry to get a bottle of plonk. Even then Fatso turned his nose up at it because it was in a box, leaving yours truly to finish off the rest of the three litres single-handed, because once you've opened one of those things they go off in a matter of hours. Anyway that's not the

41

kind of spirit that's going to sweep the country, and in my view they'd have done better to join the Libs and stop farting about.

M. is very much over the moon about Farmer Jim Prior. Do you remember him? Red faced party with a slight look of Sailor Ted, always bowling Margaret googlies in the House on the economic wicket, sent off to Siberia i.e. Belfast where the signs are he is sinking rapidly down the Bog, unlikely to leave so much as a trace behind. The latest wheeze was to hand over some degree of autonomy to the natives, but come election day they voted in the local Mau Mau, though what else they expected I haven't a blind idea. I do rather harp on this, Bill, but the sooner quite frankly we hand it all over to that little rogue Haughey and let him have a go the better! Can't think what they've got against the Micks. You and I have been over to Dublin in the past — you remember the episode of the Major's mother in the Shelbourne, or was it the second Mrs Picarda? Anyway no matter — and have many happy memories. Prods and Left Footers co-habiting in a perfectly civilised way, rain bucketing down, sod all else to do but drink. A fairly high rate of insanity, of course, but who are we to talk? Looking around my immediate circle I realise what they say about mental illness affecting one in three is probably putting it pretty mildly. You and I should count ourselves damn lucky we've escaped thus far. I don't know if I told you about conditions in Podmore's bin in Hove and that's meant to be run on liberal lines. But I digress.

I shall do my damnedest to get down to the Major's Firework Party on Saturday night. Tell him I did ask little Nott to bring back a supply of Argie thunder-flashes from his Falklands trip, but he let me down as per usual, and all I got was a Union Jack teacosy knitted by some superannuated Widow Sheepshagger. We could throw that on the bonfire I suppose. For God's sake restrain Maurice P from bringing his patent firework-lighter again. The insurance people still haven't paid for his flat.

Yours till Gibraltar crumbles,

DENIS

10 Downing Street
Whitehall

Dear Bill,

I expect you heard the news about old Leonid B. turning his toes up at long last. Boris was very cut up about it and wanted me to put the flag at half mast but the Boss vetoed the suggestion. She's been in a black anti-Russian mood all week over this latest spy chappie being caught with his pants down in Cheltenham. I wasn't a bit surprised myself as it's always been my view that those secrets johnnies are perverts and weirdoes to a man, witness that friend of the Major's who was something very hush hush and used to dress up in women's clothes until the police caught him interfering with a traffic warden in Dorking. Ah well. Still, it seems a bit stiff giving old Prime 35 years when if you slaughter your missus with a meat cleaver all you get is a ticking off from the beak on the grounds that Willie Whitelaw hasn't got sufficient accommodation available in the Scrubs.

Re. the latest election plans, I don't know if I've ever told you about Margaret's South African Guru, a chap called Van der Pump who lives up a flag pole somewhere on the East Coast. He really is a most extraordinary little cove. He's spent most of his life, as far as I can piece together from what he has told me, roughing it with the pygmies. According to Van der P. they can fill their bums with water like camels' humps and walk across the desert for days on end. I don't believe a word of it myself, but that is one of the yarns he spins. The Boss is frightfully impressed, along with the Heir to the Throne, who has appointed Van der P. Godfather of the Royal brat.

This old S. African johnny, who was very thick with Mountbatten by the way (and take that as you like it), is a great believer in dreams, and if he's had pickled onions the night before you can bet your bottom dollar he'll be on the blower at dawn holding forth with a message for the nation. During the Falklands Show he was constantly hogging the hot line to Margaret. I remember on one occasion he'd had a dream about a bear eating his trousers while he was in the bath, and when he took a shotgun to it the bear gave them back neatly pressed and wrapped up in one of those plastic bags you get

from the dry cleaners. This, according to Van der P., was obviously a signal to send off the Task Force and blow hell out of the bear, i.e. Johnny Argie. I said to Margaret at the time I thought this was pretty daft as the Task Force had left some weeks before, and asked her if she'd like to hear a dream I'd had about me and Maurice stuck up a tree at Worplesdon with Fatty Soames driving an ice-cream cart round and round the trunk. This only elicited a frosty look from M. and it was clear that Van der P's effort was a clear winner in the dream stakes.

Anyway, M. being away getting to know Herr Schidt's successor, ludicrously enough called Herr Coal — though Germans always have pretty peculiar names in my experience, and good riddance en passant to that ghastly old snuff-taker in the sailor hat — when blow me, Van der P. comes through on the scrambler with the latest news from the world of the subconscious. Having retired to bed after a fairly fierce curry at the local Khyber Pass, the old boy had nodded off and found himself alone in a strange landscape thickly wooded with banana trees. Judge of his surprise when a huge owl fluttered down, bearing in its talons an alarm clock. I stopped listening at this point, being rather preoccupied with the Daily Telegraph crossword puzzle, but anyway the message I was to give the Proprietor on her return was to go for a snap Autumn election in 83. He repeated it several times, obviously thinking I was half cut, which I was, and wouldn't remember to put it on the Memo P, which I didn't.

Anyway the Suffolk Soothsayer has had his way and the Cabinet have been told to clear their desks in preparation for all-out war with Worzel in nine months time.

I find it hard to disentangle M's thinking on strategy, but according to Boris the scheme is to flog off the North Sea, British Rail and the BBC to the small punter in the interim. So tell that broker of yours — Meinerzhagen? Fellowes? anyway no matter — to get off his fat arse and beatle down to the Exchange before all the Japs get in on the act. Brother Howe has been told to pull a few rabbits out of his hat come budget day, and then they plan to stand back and watch while poor old Gummidge falls to bits, the Boss romping home on the You Know it Makes Sense ticket. A pretty grim prospect, what? Another four years in Colditz for Yours Truly could bring about his premature demise, what with the medicinal intake necessary to see one through the stresses and strains, lack of conviviality with old chummoes, constant exposure to frightful Euros, Wogs, Orientals etc.

A propos Maurice, the whole Picbrick thing has blown up in his face as I predicted, taking with it a good deal of the Major's diligently accumulated pile. You may remember lunch at the RAC some months ago with the wordless Dane, when they all got carried away by the technicolour brochure. Of course it now turns out that Per Olaffsen, amusing drinking companion though he was, had failed to obtain the patent, and that his original scheme for compressing old copies of the Daily Telegraph into handy building blocks bore a striking resemblance to one being marketed in Reading by a subsidiary of General Motors. Writs showered down like autumn leaves on the wretched Maurice, Olaffsen having by this stage done a bunk to South Africa, and there is now talk of the bailiffs moving in and sequestering the stall at the Antique Hypermarket that I always thought belonged to his WVS lady with the smudged lipstick and the pekinese. All this bodes ill, I fear, for our friend's fragile sanity. The medics warned me when they let him out last time that there could be a yo-yo effect in terms of a rapid return to the bin unless any sort of stress was steered well clear of.

Dos vidanya!

DENIS

10 Downing Street
Whitehall

Dear Bill,

Do please thank your people at Inter-drink for the consignment of Yuletide hooch. As you probably know official policy is that all unsolicited gifts are strictly verboten, but in this case, I thought I would make an exception. Alas, the Aspreys Gold Cocktail Cabinet and Video from Maurice's friend who is trying to break into House of Commons catering has had to go back, as the delivery people made themselves rather conspicuous at the front door.

Good news on the Interest front. Little Furniss at the Natwest was on the blower in a trice offering a very nice mark-up on their new Golden Bond scheme. Howe, it seems, rather overdid it with his slashing rates to revitalise the economy wheeze: the pound was dribbling away to virtually nothing against all other currencies, so M. had no alternative but to hike the interest rates back up to a level more acceptable to the small investor such as you and I, the little bit extra coming in very handy at this time of the year.

How much longer poor old Willie Whitelaw can stay in one piece is anybody's guess. That awful little Trot with the moustache Livingstone had, it seems, invited the IRA's Top Brass over for a beano at the County Hall, and naturally Worzel, seeing the moderate vote slipping through his fingers yet again, was hopping mad. This was obviously pissing in the wind as far as Comrade Ken was concerned, even after the Bogtrotters had gone on a further rampage by way of celebration. General uproar, call for immediate debagging and Cherry Blossom treatment for the County Hall Commissar, invitations to be rescinded forthwith. Two fingers from the South Bank, Red K in no mood to argue. It therefore fell to our fat friend at the Home Office to play the man.

Whitelaw, as I may have said before, is the kind of chap who has to look up his arse to see if he's got his hat on, though perfectly decent with it and a pleasant golfing companion. It turned out anyway that he had shared the salt with the same bloodstained men of violence way back in the old days when he was Our Man in the Bogs, so who was he to say they couldn't come over? It was pathetic, quite frankly, Bill, to hear the poor old boy puffing and spluttering like some great water-buffalo trying to talk his way out of this one: Boris and I happened to be outside the door, sampling a noggin or twain of your friend's Sloe Gin, and our hearts went out to him. Was he a man or a mouse, thank goodness he hadn't had anything to do with the Falklands otherwise we'd have no navy left, no wonder old ladies can't jog across Wandsworth Common without being hit over the head, couldn't he spend a week with her Swiss Dentist or at least do something about his dandruff? In the end Whitelaw staggered out looking like a beanbag run over by a juggernaut, and half an hour later they issued a statement banning the Sinn Fein from setting foot on the Septic Isle. Needless to say Whitelaw immediately in the firing line from all and sundry: banning the buggers is playing into hands of extremists, making martyrs, just what they want, why didn't he sod off back to his pigfarm in Cumbria. (All of which I happen to agree with, but don't for God's sake quote me.)

The other person who turned up like a bad penny the other morning was little Peter Carrington, looking bronzed and sleek, now working for some very top-drawer money-lending outfit in the City. Boss pretty cool, what the hell did he want, she very busy woman etc. It turns out Peter C. had come hot foot from the sticky end of the Med, bringing tidings from the Chief Wog. All the Sons of the Desert, dirty little buggers as you and I from long experience know them to be, have got their Allah-catchers in a twist about the Boss refusing to extend the paw of friendship to one of Arafat's swarthy side-kicks at present free-loading his way round the diplomatic circuit, cocktails with old Hopalong etc. Fears according to P.C. rife among the usurers of EC1 that this could mean a re-run of the Death of a Princess episode, honeypot snatched from their sticky little hands and so forth. After about five minutes of the cuff-shooting and tie straightening, Carrington got the Whitelaw treatment with a suddenness and ferocity that surprised even me. Our aristocratic friend's role in the Argentine Invasion needless to say not being forgotten.

A propos, the Proprietor presses ahead with her plans for a State Visit to the Sheepshaggers, undeterred by wiser voices drawing attention to the hazards involved, i.e. twenty-six hour non-stop flight in World War Two Halifax, constant mid-air refuelling by breeches buoy, Argie kami-kaze wallahs whizzing to and fro, no in-flight Duty Free, which rules me out for a start, and the grisliest of accommodation waiting at the Upland Goose; shades of the Tamanrasset Hilton, not to mention unexploded bombs in the khazi and other hazards to walkabout. They have now decided in their infinite wisdom to pour another thirty-one million quid down the drain on 'developing' the rock-strewn South Atlantic Wilderness. Even Maurice Picarda after a heavy session at the RAC the other night couldn't get excited about the business prospects down there. According to one ex-Sheepshagger who lives just down the road from him in Sevenoaks, double-glazing blows out before you can put it in, and solar heating is something of a dead duck as the sun only shines three days a year.

What are your Xmas schemes? I've already posed beside the Tree for publicity purposes and that, as far as I am concerned, will be my sole contribution. The Major's travel agent friend has come up with five nights in Sidi Birani for £45, which seems very good value, even though they've only got a nine-hole course. Would Daphne pick up the tab?

Yours in hope,

DENIS

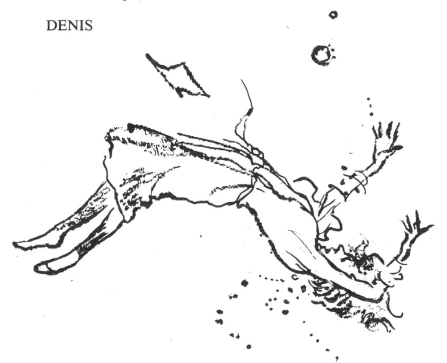

Dear Bill,

By the time the idle yobboes at British Telecom or whatever they call postmen nowadays have got round to delivering this I imagine you will be back from five nights of invigorating North African sunshine and ready to look the New Year in the face. The nearest I got to a trip abroad was the Red Star Delivery to Northern Ireland and back as part of the Boss's pre-Christmas morale boosting whistletop tour of the front line. I must say, Bill, the old peace-and-good-will-to-all-men sounded a bit thin when relayed over the Bogside to the accompaniment of exploding cars and the rattle of small-arms fire courtesy the Shamrock League of New York. Saatchis seemed very satisfied with the whole exercise, but personally I felt a bit of a mutt traipsing round the hospitals in the Royal wake with Margaret doing her Florence Nightingale act for the TV cameras. Quite honestly, Bill, if you'd just been blown up by the IRA and were lying there listening to Radio One on the earphones, would the sight of the Proprietor attended by Yours Truly plus a bevy of brasshats and reptiles all bearing down on you with a lot of damnfool questions like "How are you feeling now?" do much to promote a swift recovery?

I had a word with poor old Prior while we were being shunted up in the Laundry Lift for Security Reasons, and he said the whole thing was a nightmare. No sooner talk a bit of sense into one side than the other lot of mad bogtrotters start jumping up and down howling for the death of King James the First or some mediaeval Pope, and as for the talk of Margaret "getting on top of the gunmen" when we've got several battalions of our own constantly inflaming the Left Footers with the Knock on the Door in the Night she might as well whistle for the wind. I always find the old Farmer a trifle hard to understand, but when he tried to outline his schemes for a new Talking Shop I found the glazing over processes began to operate instantly, and I had to pop behind a trolley of soiled laundry for First Aid from the hipflask.

Meanwhile here at Chequers a mood of solemn despair reigns in all quarters. Clearly scenting a free beano, Mark turned on Christmas Eve, as usual unannounced, and offering as pretext madcap scheme to take over De Lorean Cars with funds made available by Robert Maxwell and some perfume manufacturer in Hong Kong — this inevitably going down like a cup of cold sick with the Boss. As we were trying to get ourselves into the mood for the obligatory attendance at the Midnight Service in Great Missenden I did my best to discourage him from bringing his latest belle along, a rather portly South African number who does PR work for one of those shady Save the Animals organisations the poor D of E falls for from time to time. My advice unheeded we set off four in the back seat, Mr. Wu reluctantly at the wheel, Miss Joleen bubbling noisily into a handkerchief throughout the carols and the pious words, drawing many a black glance from the Heroine of the Falklands.

What put the tin hat on it as far as I was concerned, just I had folded the specs on the bedside table at 0.15 hrs approx and composed myself for sleep, was the urgent jangling of the telephone at my ear. For a moment it crossed my befuddled mind that the Argics might be storming up the beaches at Folkestone as some kind of tit for tat, but it turned out to be the old crackpot Van der Pump, against whom Margaret will hear not a word, with his Almanack for 1983, as compiled from a recent dream. After half and hour of him crackling away into Margaret's ear about great white sheep roaming the mountains devouring everything in their path I took two pillows and slumped off to sleep on the sofa under the Christmas Tree and woke in agony from pine needle acupuncture.

Better to draw a veil over the more intimate miseries of Christmas Day. With the distant gleam of an election on the horizon, Margaret had thought up the wheeze of inviting all and sundry in for a fork lunch on Boxing Day, casting by Saatchi and Saatchi. As usual the absolute scrapings of the barrel, rather like some glorified Parky Entertainment: out of work actors, dilapidated peers of the realm, assorted odds and sods crowding round Margaret and roaring their silly heads off at her damnfool jokes, specially composed by the old fool in the dressing gown who is always wheeled in to help out on such occasions.

Meanwhile the telephone has never stopped ringing, the word having got about that the Boss is poised to reshuffle,

following the departure of that prize ass Nott, who as I have mentioned before, appears to have burned his fingers quite badly on the Rossminster business. Poor old Willie Whitelaw who had clearly been hitting it fairly hard, came through, his voice choked with sobs, convinced that he was for the chop, all he wanted to do was to retire quietly to the gun room with his Labrador and do the decent thing. I assured him the Proprietor would never hear of it. Ever since Reggie Maudling's liver came out with its hands up the Boss has looked to Willy as the last surviving relic of the Grand Old Days. This also incidentally explains why she insists on keeping on Hailsham, long after human charity would have dictated he be put out to grass at the funny farm. It makes no sense to me, Bill. M. keeps reading the Riot Act when she discovers from the Telegraph that another rapist has been let off with a caution, and who does she have in charge of law and order but two old buffers who couldn't keep the peace as night nurse in a geriatric ward.

May the great bird of the New Year let fall its blessings upon your head.

Yours aye,

DENIS

53

Dear Bill,

First things first. I wouldn't bother if I were you to go up to town for the Lillywhites sale. I had a quick whizz round en route for the Ritz Bar, and quite frankly, apart from the evil-smelling horde of Arabs hurling athletic supports from hand to hand in the jogging department there didn't seem much of interest to you. I made do with a set of thermal Japanese golf hats in pastel shades, knocked down to practically nothing. Maurice's friend with the funny leg swears by them, and I thought they might enliven the scene at Worplesdon.

You'll forgive me for not giving you prior notice of this present little excursion, but we were all sworn to keep absolutely mum, lest the Argies bomb the airstrip prior to our arrival. When it was first mooted, in company with assorted brasshats and other Whitehall buffers all drawing her attention to the various hazards attached, I wrang my hands imploring M. to think again. Pym however seemed singularly sanguine urging her to press on and fulfil her destiny. (I wonder why?).

Needless to say the Boss had her way, but agreed to throw sand in the eyes of the reptiles with talk of a cancellation, and limit the operation to an Ulster-style "inner and outer". I thought it only right and proper to motor the old girl out to Brize Norton and flutter my hanky from the waving base, telling her as she studied her red boxes in the passenger seat of my deep regrets that I couldn't come along and enjoy all the fun. After she said "But you *are* coming, Denis" for the third time the penny finally dropped and I began to feel very queasy indeed. Not only was I unsuitably accoutred for the Antarctic, but I had several dates lined up on the old While the Cat's away the Mice will play syndrome, and therefore had to ring round from the only available telephone in the Nissen Hut at the drome. All slightly embarrassing.

Next thing I know it's up a little ladder into the boneshaker, chocks away, and eyes down for seven hours hardarse non-stop to Ascension. The worse thing about it, Bill, was that not being forewarned I was deprived even of the solace of my little flask which I always pack for these occasions. I tried to light a gasper, but it was immediately knocked out of my hand by some Air Commodore, roaring above the din of the engines that I must be mad, didn't I realise I was sitting on forty thousand gallons of high octane fuel? You can imagine my mental state when we tottered out at Ascension, a godforsaken spot if I ever I saw one, or so I thought until we reached the Falklands. My hopes of a quick dash to the Duty Free were immediately put paid to as we were frog-marched up another ladder into an even older biplane, and off for another thirteen hours of unmitigated hell, teeth chattering with the vibration, as we nose-dived towards the sea to take on fuel from a stalling nuclear bomber, Margaret unruffled by it all still deep in her boxes and writing her Christmas thank-you letters.

Finally I was awakened from a nightmarish doze and hustled out into the blizzard to be met by that awful little slug Hunt, who used to be the Governor, and a small crowd of blue-nosed Sheepshaggers, the surrounding view bringing back unhappy memories of our grisly holidays with Lord Pucefeatures on the Isle of Muck. M. strides in, a dreadful gleam in her eye, and begins to press the flesh, a half-witted photographer from the local roneoed news-sheet The Shaggers' Weekly falling about in the background popping off his flashbulbs.

I think we had shaken hands with the entire population of the benighted settlement before the wretched Hunt's better half brightly announced that she had put the kettle on. We were then, if you are still with me, invited to climb into a ridiculous London taxi, and driven off through the minefield to Mon Repos, locally known as Dunshaggin. On arrival we are greeted by a smouldering peat fire, tea and rock buns arranged on tasteful doylies, whereupon Hunt, catching the light of insanity in my eye, mutters that if I like to accompany him upstairs, he has something that might interest me. This proved to be a captured pair of underpants once belonging to General Menendez, now mounted by his good lady in a pokerwork frame.

Controlling my emotions, I suggested a stroll to stretch the legs after our long ordeal. Resisting the fool Hunt's suggestion of a trek up Mount Tumbledown, I reached the Goose six minutes later, only to find the bar crammed with inebriate reptiles, brasshats, airline stewards and one or two cross-eyed Sheepshaggers of idiotic mien sitting in a corner reminiscing gloomily about the good old days under the Argies when at least they could get a drink.

As I write our time of departure is still very much under wraps, Margaret having toddled off to a small thanksgiving service at the local tin tabernacle and showing every desire to stay on indefinitely. At least, thanks to Mine Host, Bill Voletrouser, I am now well prepared for the return trip, a miniature in every pocket and a fire extinguisher full of the amber fluid for discreet in-flight refuelling.

Yours in transit

DENIS

Dear Bill,

I'm sorry I had to miss Podmore's seventieth birthday celebrations but I was still pretty flaked out with Shag Lag. I had in fact to be brought back from Brize Norton on a stretcher, rigor having set in somewhere over Ascension, and Dr. O'Gooley who was summoned round by the Boss diagnosed severe stress complicated by dehydration. I then swallowed a handful of brown bombers, washed down with your generous two-litre bottle of Bells with the handle on the side and was unconscious for seventy two hours.

I woke up fresh as a daisy to find that Wonderwoman had meanwhile zapped the Bank of England, bollocked the Usurers, and propped up the pound with one hand while blaming it all on that seedy little man with the pot belly and the quiff, Peter Shore, who had taken advantage of her absence to spread panic and despondency.

Our lot are tremendously cock a hoop about the Report on the Falklands. I don't know if I've mentioned him, but Margaret has this dogsbody called Gow, a bald, chubby, brown-tongued little fellow from somewhere on the South Coast, what the Yanks call a gopher, i.e. gopher this, gopher that, usually M's handbag. Anyway this prancing pixie was duly dispatched to the newsagents to bring back an armful on the morning after Franks hit the stands: surprise surprise Maggie Not To Blame, P. Carrington perfectly nice little man and only doing his best, poor old Nott much maligned — you may see that Lazards have taken him on board at forty grand a year, so much for the back to the daffodil farm routine, what? — F.O. going through all the necessary motions to the best of their ability.

Implausible as all this might seem it came as no surprise to me. Franks, you may not know, is One of Them, having done time as Our Man in Washington before bumbling off to spend his twilight years being Professor Branestawm among the dreaming spires. It was hardly to be expected therefore that this old boffin would name the Guilty Men, i.e. the FO, a nest of every conceivable variety of pinko, queer, Trot and deviant known to medical science, each one of them ready at the drop of a nicker to sell us down the river to any foreign swine that hoves into view, be it Galtieri, Andropov or Chu Chin Chow.

Whatever reservations I may have had however were as naught to the consternation at Smellysocks House. Worzel and his cohorts, who have been going through a baddish patch these last few years, had been pinning their hopes on Comrade Franks doling out a goodly quota of mud to fling at the Boss. As dawn broke on publication day they were therefore to be seen eagerly queuing outside the Stationery Office, clutching in their sweaty palms the seventeen pounds fifty necessary to secure a copy. Holborn then crowded with malodorous men in dirty raincoats hastily thumbing their way to page 506 where His Lordship finally concludes "I therefore lay the blame entirely on the Argies." Clatter of dentures on the pavement, collapse of elderly parties. How now to spin out four-day emergency debate demanded by Worzel in first flush of excitement?

Talking of derelicts, who should I see weaving his way along Whitehall the other morning at a very unsocial hour but M. Picarda, en route for a Mass Rally of the Faithful at Temperance Hall to relaunch the Alliance, which as you may not have noticed has been aground for some months. As I told him they could hardly have chosen a worse moment with the Boss rapidly climbing back into the charts following her ENSA tour of the Minefields. How hiring the Temperance Hall and wheeling out Ol' Foureyes is going to help their cause I have no idea. Maurice himself seems to have a shrewder grasp of how to woo Johnny Public. He tells me he has booked an upstairs room at a pub in Sevenoaks to revive his own local prospects, and has already engaged the services of two strippers. His son by his first marriage has formed a pop group and threatens to participate. I agree it sounds absolutely grisly but I did promise to show my face, weather permitting, and throw a bread roll or two. Any chance of your being let off the leash?

Yours in anticipation,

DENIS

Dear Bill,

So sorry you couldn't make it to Maurice's little S.D.P. shinding at the Pig and Leper in Sevenoaks. As I feared, things got rather out of hand. Maurice's first born, he of the aquamarine cockatoo haircut and leather three-piece suit, created such a din with his amplified electric banjos before passing out under the influence of Uhu that one couldn't really hear oneself speak. Maurice was still very shaky after his release on parole from the bin, and apologised for having to touch us for our drinks as we arrived. By the time the sticky stage was reached the old boy had become very morose and began to malign his leader, saying that Brer Jenkins had led them into a quagmire and was all piss and wind, and that the Doctor chap with the Brylcreemed hair and the shifty eyes was about as much use as a rubber johnny dispenser at the Vatican. Whether or not he will join various other deadbeats in creeping back into the fold remains to be seen.

I had a very merry little mid-morning snorterino with my bald friend Furniss, the Manager down at the local Branch of the NatWest. He was fair carolling with glee at the news that surprise surprise Howe proposes to distribute largesse to all and sundry in his forthcoming budget. How was it possible, the gleaming-pated little banker enquired, when only a few weeks ago there had been nothing but gloomy talk of sinking pounds, rising interest rates and the imperative need for the lower paid to tighten their belts in the interests of national survival?

It is quite extraordinary how thick your average bank-manager can be, though of course I didn't say so. Over a further largish dose of his disgusting sherry I patiently explained the rules of play. Come election time, big talk from party in power about currying no favour with electorate, we shall not be deflected from our high mission, noble ideals cannot be sacrificed for temporary popularity at the booths etc etc closely followed by massive bribes to every man jack of the community, Howe no exception to long line of shysters in high office.

Encouraged by little Furniss's gleaming eyes and dog-like admiration at my grasp of world affairs, I moved on to a tour d'horizon of the Middle East. Taking that little bearded bugger. Sheikh Yamani-oryalife, as my starting point, I unfolded to my spellbound audience of one how it was that brother Wog got us all into this god-awful mess in the first place by multiplying the price of oil by any figure that came into his fuzzy little head, thus bringing in train the more distressing aspects of inflation, rocketing price of booze etc. Close on his heels, I explained, drawing a rough graph on his desk with a finger moistened with Amontillado, follows Mass Recession. Comes the time jalopies all over the Western world grind to a halt, owners take to push-bike. Oil-producing Coons begin to squeal. White Massah no buy Magic Black Treacle. Eventually fragile unity of dusky-hued oil-producers breaks up in confusion, craftier Coons offer Magic Black Treacle under counter White Massah very good price. Brother Wog bites dust, general rejoicing, save for the likes of Carrington and D. Hurd who now see many years of exercising the brown-coated tongue to have been of no avail. By the end of this, Furniss was in tears, kissed me on both cheeks and agreed to advance me fifty thou to put on the gee-gees any time I felt like a flutter.

A propos the Waterworkers' Strike. My withers were wrung by your account of having to boil water from old mother Wheatcroft's pump down in the village, but as you never touch the stuff they did not remain wrung for any length of time. There's certainly no point in your coming up to Downing Street for a bath as you suggest. If it's any comfort to you, the Boss and Tebbit are confident that in a day or so the Shitshovellers will have run up the flag and come out of the sewers with their hands up. If the present dispute has proved anything, it is that these layabouts are obviously surplus to requirements and should count themselves damn lucky to be drawing a regular pay-packet, albeit slightly soiled, when most of the rest of us are on the dole.

Here's a tip from the horse's mouth. Don't be surprised should Hopalong drop off the perch. We're knee-deep here in publicity bumf from his equivalent of the Saatchi Twins, telling us that despite his advanced years he has never felt fitter, enjoys eight hours uninterrupted sleep a day and waterworks in perfect order. I always said he'd never make old bones.

Yours affectionately

DENIS

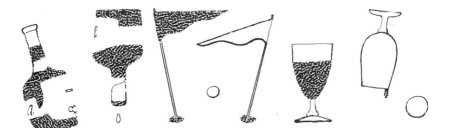

10 Downing Street
Whitehall

25 FEBRUARY 1983

Dear Bill,

By the time this reaches you the fartarsing-about down in Bermondsey will be over, and in any case the result will in no way dent the rising line of Margaret's graph, which seems set fair to go off the top of the board with an all-Tory House of Commons as soon as she blows the necessary whistle. Boris says it'll be June according to the Kremlin, but they don't always know. The thinking, according to him is that the inflation will be down to four per cent by the summer, and before it roars off into double figures again in the autumn they can go to the hustings with a lot of flashy talk on the lines of look what we've done. In fact, as you and I know perfectly well, it's sod all to do with M's mob and is fixed by a lot of greasy little money-lenders over in Wall Street, but obviously nobody can say that in public.

Not surprisingly, spirits over at Smellysocks House have hit an all-time low, and the horny-handed sons of toil are beginning, albeit slow-wittedly, to move towards the idea of an Ides of March scenario for Worzelius Tribune of the Plebs. Picture the scene, Bill, as the poor old buffer shuffles down to the Senate, his ill-fitting toga flapping in the breeze. Enter R. and L. assorted malodorous conspirators, Wedgius Lunaticus in the van, Healius of the interwoven eyebrows, Tatchellus Arsebandicus in minitoga bringing up the rear. Then, as the white-haired loon paused to expectorate across the Forum the H of C cutlery flashes in the air, and the poor old bibliophile slips with scarce a groan to the garbage-littered pavement. This, I should say, is the one thing our lot dread like poison, for fear of what may follow after, though quite frankly, Bill, the idea of that pot-bellied scruff Shore, let alone Old Swiveleyes Benn marshalling a force to be reckoned with seems to me fairly remote.

The only cloudlet on the horizon at our end has been the latest in a long line of leaks — the Trots of the Civil Service if you ask me. Among the motley train of courtiers, hairdressers, speechwriters, Sir Custardface in the Dressing Gown, old Uncle Van der Pump and all, I don't know if I have drawn your attention to a rubicund egghead in early middle age of the unlikely name of Bertram Mount, known to his intimates as Bertie. A few months ago he was rescued from the morass of unemployment and given some kind of desk job in the basement by little Gow, adding the odd intellectual thought to the Boss's harangues. Finding himself, like all these supernumeraries, with a good deal of time on his hands, he was detailed off by the Boss to go away and dream up a few five-year plans in case they got in again and had to do something. (Apparently Winston used to do that sort of thing, employing bright young men like Harold Macmillan to brood in the library and submit their suggestions on a postcard please to Number Ten.)

Anyway, Bill, to cut a long story short, young Mount, being something of a swat, toddles round, stopping all and sundry in the corridors of power, Tebbit, Howe, the Monk etc., asking them a lot of damnfool questions like they do at airports, about where they thought the country should be heading in the nineties. This inevitably produced a flood of unhinged and visionary gibberish, especially from the Monk, who fancies himself as something of a Seer. I even got in on the act, trapped by young Bertie en route for the cellar, and as I had already had quite a few, was only too happy to oblige. The resulting folder was handed into the Boss's office last week. Boris had it photocopied and it seemed to me to be a right load of codswallop. Everyone, surprise surprise, to stand on their own feet, crack down on Women's Lib, Asian millionaires to be held up as exemplars to benighted blackamoors as the way out of rat-infested ghettoes, Sunday School to be made compulsory but taken out of hands of C of E Pinkoes, Ma Whitehouse into Cabinet as Minister of Arts etc.

Next morning, inevitably, all this rubbish is splashed comma for comma across the Guardian. Feeble show of indignation from Smelly Socks Brigade, interpreting Master Bertie's milksop measures as a full-scale return to Victorian Britain. Would that it were.

Needless to say, my own more down-to-earth and practical ideas i.e. Passports for all Paddies, Privatise the BBC, Flogging for Muggers, Whitelaw out to Grass, Tax-free Booze, Prison for Poofs, Fathers not responsible for Sons' Debts or Sons in any way after age of twelve — were not deemed worthy of inclusion, as per usual.

Will you tell Daphne I can't give away the prizes at her Disabled Jockeys Ball, as I promised Squiffy's Sawbones friend in the North I'd slip into the bib and tucker and offer myself for target practice to the Hibernian bread roll hurlers at Carnoustie, who have very generously volunteered to make me an Honorary Member of their club, free set of Jap irons and a couple of crates of Glen Kamikaze thrown in.

Yours in haste,

DENIS

10 Downing Street
Whitehall
11 MARCH 1983

Dear Bill,

Thank you for ringing me up to tell me I was on the telly the other evening. By the time I got to the screen, inevitably, it was all over, but Boris seemed very amused and toasted my driving ability in his mother's 1982 plum vodka. Trust the reptiles to try and make me look a BF, and succeed by all accounts.

Ever since the Metro launch in Birmingham a couple of years back, the Boss has had a soft spot for the shower up at British Leyland, and despite my continued harping on what happened to poor Maurice Picarda when the steering wheel of his Metro came away in his hands as he was going the wrong way down the M4 after that Masonic shindig at Chippenham, she continues to lend her name to promoting their ramshackle assemblages of cheap scrap-iron. The latest British-built number, indistinguishable as far as I could tell from any of the little Jap runabouts the Major's friend sells down at Tunbridge Wells at half the price, was brought to the door by their PR man, an oily little greaser by the name of Smythe-Pemberton, who claimed to be a friend of Squiffy's. All over the proprietor with his sales talk, reclining ashtrays, digital rear wipers, swivelling sidelights etc., immediate delivery six months to a year. Boss then stage-managed out onto the doorstep, all

aglow with wonder at latest triumph of British knowhow —
I'm told the engine, by the by, is eighty-five per cent built in
Taiwan — reptiles seven deep on the pavement, obediently
recording the event with popping flashbulbs, whirr of cameras,
etc. M. jumps in, poses with arm upraised in royal wave, and
purrs effortlessly away from kerb for one minute thirty-second
test drive. Wonderful, marvellous, now it's your turn Denis.

As it was by now half-past ten in the morning, I had taken a
couple of large ones on board, and strode forward to play my
part in the Birth of the Boom. Slammed door, turned key in
ignition, foot down, and off we shot. As the reptiles scattered,
a woman apparently sitting in the back seat told me to fasten
my seatbelt. I turned round, Bill, and would you believe it?
Not a soul in sight. Gave me a pretty nasty turn, I don't mind
telling you. Brakes on, beads of sweat forming on the
forehead, is this a return of the old trouble, pink spiders up the
wall etc? Bring vehicle to shaky stop alongside the kerb,
narrowly missing Smythe-Pemberton's Lamborghini, very
badly parked incidentally, whatever they may have said, and
eject from vehicle to cries of "Good old Denis!" and guffaws
of laughter from the various flag-waving yobboes and
charladies who hang about in Downing Street with nothing
better to do. Smythe-Pemberton explained later that all these
kamikaze jobs are fitted with an I-speak-your-Weight device
that reminds you to empty the ashtrays and so forth as a sales
gimmick. I said it seemed a damn fool idea to me and could
cause a lot of accidents.

Otherwise, as you have probably seen from the Telegraph,
M. is shaping up for another twenty-eight round bout with
King Arthur, the Beast of Barnsley. She was bloody livid when
the Water Board caved in and gave the shit shovellers twelve
per cent, and now the message is a fight to the death with any
section of the Smelly Socks Contingent that appears on any
pretext whatsoever. So Tebbit has been ordered off to draw up
a new rule-book in his painstaking handwriting which will
involve an absolute ban on any industrial action whatsoever in
the service industries a la Jaruzelski. Margaret has also
whistled up one of her geriatric Yanks called Mr. MacGregor,
responsible for liquidating British Steel, to have a crack at
closing down (a) NCB, and (b) BR, thus leaving the way clear
for British Leyland and their rotten little cars to swarm all over
the country unimpeded.

What of Worzelius, you may ask? Ides of March scenario, like everything else organised by Smellysocks House, an absolute cock-up. Worzelius alerted to the raised daggers by the reptiles, leaving the conspirators to resheathe the knives and forks and explain on TV how loyal they were to the old party, heaven forfend that any of his white hairs should be harmed etc. The day of reckoning in other words now postponed till after Darlington, much to the relief, I should say, of our side, who had been dreading the spectre of an Opposition with Koalaface in charge.

I gather Maurice P. is on something of a high following the bum's rush administered to young Tatchell by the good burghers of Bermondsey. The Sevenoaks SDP immediately doubled their membership to eight, and Picarda finished up in the cells after overdoing the victory celebrations and writing off the garage. Did the Major ring you about Venice? Seemed a damn stupid idea to me. Squiffy was very scornful. Apparently they had a reps' conference there in November, and those that didn't go down with Montezuma's revenge walked out of the hotel after dinner and fell in the lake.

Do give us a bell if you have any better ideas. This time ideally not after one a.m.

Hasta la vista.

DENIS

66

10 Downing Street
Whitehall

25 MARCH 1983

Dear Bill,

I couldn't agree with you more about friend Howe's abysmal performance with the tattered red box. The reptiles did their best to make it look as though all of us on over fifty thou were going to clean up, but I've done my sums and what with the 25p on my morning bottle of the hard stuff, fags up yet again, and 4p extra on juice for the Roller, I should say we were roughly speaking back where we started from, i.e. despite little Howe's giddy trigonometry, $x = 0$.

This, from where I sit, is not the stuff to give the troops on the eve of the great battle with Worzelius, whensoever M. in her infinite wisdom decides to fire the first cannonade. In any case the idea of that crepe-soled little creep, Brer Howe, the so-called Mogadon Man, giving us the Gentlemen of England Now In Bed speech from Henry the Fifth, would seem to smack of brainstorms in the casting department.

The only social event in my calendar of late was a little bachelor dinner-party I gave at Number Ten, in the Proprietor's absence on the hustings. Guests were Furniss and Maurice P., who is looking for a loan to start up a new data display telemessage scheme with hardware from North Korea to be assembled in a still unbuilt factory in Midlothian. I didn't entirely haul in the nuts and bolts, but the general idea is that you'll be able to punch up personal messages on the other fellow's TV screen while he's watching Coronation Street, and if he's got the right equipment he'll be able to punch one back. Sounds a damn silly idea to me, and I asked Maurice before our friend from the NatWest arrived whether it wouldn't be easier to use the old steam telephone. No, no, says he, and gives me a lot of hard sell stuff about the wave of the future, in a few years we'll all be doing the laundry, ordering rounds of drinks, playing golf etc without ever getting out of our armchairs. It was at this juncture that Boris padded in with the Supermarket sherry, Il Malodoroso, to announce that the Man from the NatWest had arrived and was being positively frisked.

I don't, Bill, know if you 'ave ever entertained your bank manager, but the first hour or so was extremely sticky. Poor Furniss was clearly rather overwhelmed at being confronted with the Seat of Power, and spent a good deal of time fingering his tie and gazing about him with a wild surmise, like the fellow standing on the peke. Maurice, never one for the finer points of etiquette and well afloat on several schooners of his preferred firewater, immediately launched into his One Hundred Good Reasons Why the NatWest Would be Mad to Miss the PicaTel Personalised Interface System Bandwagon While It Was Still At the Drawingboard Stage. As usual with Maurice, however, there came a point midway through Boris's Avocado and Baby Clam Cocktail where he ground to a halt and the glazed look, well-known to you and me, came down like dusk on Ben Lomond.

Furniss, who seemed grateful for a lull, now broadened the horizon somewhat to include the economy as a whole. He was not inclined to agree with me a propos the bespectacled swot Howe, and opined that it was all to do with the wily little Middle Eastern buggers recently in conclave at the Intercontinental Hotel — the notorious OPEC. Crikey Bill, can you imagine the camel droppings and general filth that lot left behind! I can only presume they had to hose down the rooms, but no matter. Since our last meeting Furniss had been to a seminar at Great Malvern for NatWest men at branch level, and had at last gained some insight into the balls up his lot are making of it. Interrupted only by the odd eructation or snort of dismay from Maurice, our balding friend proceeded to unfold a tale of quite frightful hard luck. While you or I, Bill, might well be rubbing our hands at the prospect of a tumble in prices at the pumps, these fat cat money-lenders have got their knickers in a real knot. Having lent all our hard-earned deposits to a gaggle of excitable South Americans and Middle Europeans, who have predictably blown it all on wine, women and song, they now foresee with some dismay the future oil-wealth of this merry gipsy band knocked down to clear at give-away prices, and the ensuring spectre of El Officiale Receibador coming in to liquidise them.

As I have been warning them of this at fifty decibels for the last two years, I could hardly forbear to crow. What alarms me, though, as I tried to explain above the snores, Maurice by now having his head down in what was left of the Avocado, is that who do we have holding our well-thumbed hand of cards in this sleazy poker-game but that prize twat Nicely Nicely Lawson, ex-reptile and property speculator? If it's left to Brother Nigel to fumble the next move, the days separating us all from the Distressed Gentlefolks Twilight Home may well be numbered on the fingers of one hand.

Head above the clouds, however, the Boss remains unperturbed. With that mule-like obstinacy I have come to know in private life for over a quarter of a century now, her new wheeze is to promote the hoary old Mastermind MacGregor to take over the pits, give little Scargill's balls a tweak, block up all the coalmines, and then get to work on dismantling British Rail. Margaret has always preferred a gas fire and has never been on a train in her life unless forced to do so. As for that little greaser Parker, she can't wait to have him broken up for scrap. This is what she calls long term strategy, though if you ask me they'll get poor little Howe pissed in the summer and wheel him out with the bribes prior to going for gold in October.

Sorry to miss you at the Worshipful Company of Spoonbenders. I would have given a lot to see the Major being given the bum's rush by the Security Wallahs. Full marks to him for pulling the Lord Mayor's head through his hat before they got to him.

Yours aye,

DENIS

10 Downing Street
Whitehall

Dear Bill,

You will forgive the somewhat unseemly gales of laughter and cracking of champagne corks when you were kind enough to ring the other evening after the Darlington show. Spirits were pretty high at this end, and we didn't find Whitelaw till the next morning. Why, you may ask, this merrymaking after a stunning defeat? Answer not far to seek. Having got their long johns in one hell of a tangle at the prospect of Koala-features Healey leading the Smellysocks into battle come the big day, the re-emergence of Worzelius Senex as the dynamic champion of the plebs inevitably produced unbridled sighs of relief.

Worzelius himself was obviously a bit carried away to boot. No sooner had he held the bespectacled Labour victor's hands over his head, than he was up on his soapbox, finger wagging and white locks adrift in the March gales, to lash out at the Boss, describing her as a heartless Victorian mill-owner seeking a return to the good old days, pushing half-grown schoolchildren up chimneys, driving the unemployed into the workhouse, and shackling feminists together to the kitchen sink. As you know, Bill, I'm not a man to sit there and have my wife insulted, and I drafted a few pretty pithy lines as the basis for a reply, dwelling with particular emphasis on the size of Red Ken's weekly inducements from the Moscow Norodny Bank, well-authenticated medical evidence from Broadmoor about Wedgwood Benn, and the ever-increasing strangle-hold of perverts of every kind on the once respectable Labour Party. The powers that be, however, to wit the Corsican Brothers Saatchi and Saatchi decreed that a dignified silence was the most telling response pro tem.

Not content with his nose-thumbing, Worzelius then wheeled out the whole party propaganda machine and produced his Blueprint for Disaster. According to Boris, who had obtained an advance copy from the printers, it got a good write-up in Pravda, and I'm not surprised. All hereditary peers into the tumbril — jolly good idea entre nous, but not good form to say so on our side — abolish the public schools — again not wholly unjustifiable, in view of what Harrow did for the half-wit Mark — all foxhunters to be shot on sight — so far so good, you may say. I never had any time for those snobby buggers in top hats and fancy dress ploughing up the countryside: why can't they play a bit of golf if they want to get some exercise? As if this is not enough, the senile Bibliophile then proposes the root and branch destruction of E. Heath's Common Market Farrago and instant withdrawal. Much to be said for this as I think you will agree. In fact, after a few sharp ones with Boris, I took the liberty of suggesting to the Proprietor that it might not be a bad wheeze to steal the old boy's clothes right down to the spats. This went down like a mug of cold sick, I need hardly add, and I was ordered to bring in eight sacks of Coalite, a gift from the Sheepshaggers, that had been dumped at the bottom of the garden.

However, Margaret obviously still felt like letting off a bit more steam. I told you about our publicity stunt to launch the so-called Maestro. Well, as I explained at the time, the motor in question is little more than a sardine box on wheels, quite apart from the Automatic Backseat Driver croaking away about seatbelts and the dangers of cigarette smoking. Scarcely has the first rickety model fallen off the assembly line and been carried cautiously away for display in the show room, than Yobs Unlimited blow the whistle and down tools all because one of their knucklebrained number had quite rightly been given the sack for fouling the back seat of an export model.

Within minutes the whole of Edwardes' so-called New Look Leyland Works is as silent as the grave, and the Longbridge mob are out in sympathy. Knowing my good lady's penchant for the little prat Edwardes and his mobile coffins, I couldn't help indulging in a spot of I-Told-You-So as the Iron Lady was scrubbing away at her newly capped incisors. Next thing M. commandeers the Jimmy Young Show to blast the Yobboes out of the water.

How was your Easter? The Major was supposed to motor over to Chequers on the Sunday to play a few holes at Streatley, prior to an extended evening at The Whistling Leper in Aston Clinton. I warned him to steer clear of Newbury in view of the massed hordes of Lesbians forming an unwashed human chain round Greenham Common, but the old boy never listens. Net result, phone call from the Clinic first thing Monday morning to say he's had another turn. Four hours stuck in the jam on the A34, dismounts to remonstrate, has all his golf clubs individually snapped for his trouble, and is lucky to get away for the price of his plus fours.

If you have time to drop in and see the old boy he's in Napley Ward, visiting hours 2pm to 2.20. No booze.

Chin chin,

DENIS

Dear Bill,

Re your coloured brochure of the Algarve 15 days half-board at the Mountbatten Motel for £143.75 including VAT for the first half of June. It all looks very enticing, I agree, and I am told by Whitelaw that the Course is a sheer delight to play on, very obliging caddies, and a nice little Englishwoman, Mrs Flack, a merry red-headed widow from Morecambe, who runs the bar.

However, as you may have gathered from the DT, there has been quite a lot talk about M. going to the Polls at that juncture, and I thought it prudent to check with Head Office before putting down the deposit. The Boss had her paperknife out, dealing with her fan-mail, and seemed in an agreeable enough mood, so I broached the vital Q. Sorry to interrupt and so forth, but any chance of a 36-hour pass come raging June? No reply. Realise it's still some time off, but in my line of business one has to plan ahead. Crippling look, ugly stabbing movement with paperknife. Feel I am now commanding her full attention, press on. Chap needs to get away from time to time, recharge the batteries, change of air, been rather on top of each other in recent months etc. M.'s eyes assume gimlet-like intensity.

I was about to come to the point and produce my Dataday, when blow me, with scarce a tap at the door, in blows little Pym. Ever since he slipped into the hastily abandoned boots of Peter C., our bespectacled friend has had the crushed and doleful mien one would expect of an ageing pugdog kept on a v. tight leash and never allowed out of its kennel except for walkies once a week, and taking a good many sly kicks into the bargain. Besides which, spending time with the poofs and closet weirdoes down at the Foreign Office have never done wonders for any normal cove's morale, witness the sad decline of his predecessor the noble peer, now, I am told, working as office boy for a firm of usurers in the City.

It transpires that Puggy P. has come hotfoot from Amman, where he has been closeted with the little bald bloke who went to Harrow some time before Mark and now runs Jordan. Old

Hopalong, when not threatening to bombard the Russkies with Death Rays from Outer Space, had cooked up some scheme to bring peace to the troubled West Bank, which had predictably fallen through, as Begin is busily occupied with building skyscrapers and Kosher Meatball Stands on every vacant lot remaining, offering cut-price mortgages to the Chosen Few through their equivalent of the Nationwide, and is about as likely to hand it back to the Arabs as Hopalong is to hand Manhatten back to the Indians. Nonetheless at his mistress's whistle, Bonzo Pym scampered off, convinced in his doggy mind that where Hopalong had failed he would succeed. Hence his gloomy expression as he now stood, hands behind his back, under the chilling gaze.

Having delivered his tidings and taken his medicine, Pym shuffled out, closing the door, leaving me to gather up the threads of my enquiry. What about it? A blank stare. Would Margaret care for a drink? Was I aware of the time? Very well, would she mind if I had one? A predictable pattern of response: she had ceased to mind years ago, if that was the way I wished to destroy what was left of my brain then I was at liberty to do so. You probably know the form; we all do. Emboldened, I returned to the fray. What price a June holiday? Could she acquaint me with her electoral intentions one way or the other as I was a busy man? At this the floodgates opened, and I was borne from the room on a tide of invective, still no wiser as I sit mournfully stabbing the Olivetti here in my little den.

As far as I can gather from Boris it all now hangs on Van der Pump, the South African seer. Her own inclination is to soldier on until the Spring, thus showing that she means business and is not one to heed the siren voices of Mori and Nop. However, should the old sage, on looking into the seaweed and consulting his stockbroker, come to the conclusion that a Bandit Raid on the electorate in June is the will of the Gods, then Bandit Raid it will be. I realise that none of this helps you much with old Mr. Vidler at the travel agent's, but I'm afraid it's the best I can do.

Should the balloon go up, the main worry on our side is that Worzelius will raise the tasteless topic of unemployment. Everyone has therefore been told to dream up ideas, under the baton of little Bertie Mount, the one-man Think Tank, and very entertaining some of them have been. The only one that has got off the ground so far is a damnfool scheme from Tarzan to recruit a kind of Heseltine Youth, equipping a select number of school leavers with old 303's, paying them half a crown a week, and marching them up and down for twelve months, with the option they can bugger off whenever they feel like it. I said why not bring back National Service and what a difference it would have made to young Mark but I got my head bitten off again, and retired hurt.

Pip pip,

DENIS